"*THIS BOOK IS SUPERB!* Few books on management are written by managers and fewer still by managers who have **succeeded** in management. There is more sense in this one small volume than in a whole library of theoretical rubbish. Mr. Townsend spares nobody, says exactly what he thinks and seldom writes an unnecessary word. Were he candidate for the Presidency of the United States he would have my vote (if I had one) and if there is a book in the world which deserves to sell a million copies, this is it."

C. Northcote Parkinson

ROBERT TOWNSEND

Robert Townsend who was born in 1920 is married, has five children and lives in Locust Valley, Long Island. He has had a distinguished business career. From 1949 he spent thirteen years as a director of the American Express Company before joining Avis Rent-a-Car Corporation in 1962. There, in three years, first as president, then as chairman, he turned this tiny company into a highly profitable, internationally respected organization. At Avis he learned, and applied, much of the wisdom contained in his book. Following his own advice he bowed out of Avis in 1965, his job completed. When he cashed his chips following his resignation, people kept asking him to help with *their* businesses. He ran out of reasons for saying "No". He wrote this book which will enable him to say, "Buy my book, take whatever you can from it, and then call me."

Up
The Organization*

***How to stop the company
stifling people and strangling profits**

Robert Townsend

CORONET BOOKS
HODDER-FAWCETT LTD

"Further Up The Organization" originally
published in the July 1970 issue of *Playboy*.
"Guerrilla Guide For Working Women"
originally published in the September 1970 issue
of *McCall's* magazine.

Printed and bound in Great Britain for
Hodder Fawcett Ltd,
St. Paul's House, Warwick Lane,
London, E.C.4
by Hazell Watson & Viney Ltd,
Aylesbury, Bucks

ISBN 0 340 14986 8

TO DON PETRIE

"And God created the Organization and gave It dominion over man."
                              Genesis 1, 30A, Subparagraph VIII

MEMORANDUM

To: *The Reader*
From: *The Author*
Subject: *How to Use* Up the Organization

This book is in alphabetical order. Using the table of contents, which doubles as the index, you can locate any subject on the list in thirteen seconds. And you can read all I have to say about it in five minutes or less.

Dip into it someplace. If you don't get at least a hollow laugh *and* a sharpened need to kick that 200-foot sponge you work for, then throw the book away. It's not for you. There are already too many organizational orthodoxies imposed on people, and I don't want to help the walking dead institute another one.

In the average company the boys in the mailroom, the president, the vice-presidents, and the girls in the steno pool have three things in common: they are docile, they are bored, and they are dull. Trapped in the pigeonholes of organizational charts, they've been made slaves to the rules of private and public hierarchies that run mindlessly on and on because nobody can change them.

So we've become a nation of office boys. Monster corporations like General Motors and monster agencies like the
Defense Department have grown like cancer until they
take up nearly all of the living working-space. Like clergy-
men in Anthony Trollope's day, we're but mortals
trained to serve immortal institutions.

This is not our natural state. Most of us come from good
solid European stock whose record of rapacity, greed,
cruelty, and treachery would make Genghis Khan look
like Mahatma Gandhi. To go down now without a whim-
per (much less a bang) is completely out of character.

Two solutions confront each of us:

Solution One *is the cop-out: you can decide that what
is must be inevitable; grab your share of the cash and
fringes; and comfort yourself with the distractions you
call leisure.*

Solution Two *is nonviolent guerrilla warfare: start dis-
mantling our organizations where we're serving them,
leaving only the parts where they're serving us. It will
take millions of such subversives to make much difference.*

This book is about Solution Two.

It's for those who have the courage, the humor, and the
energy to make a non-monster company, or a non-

---

monster piece of a monster company, operate as if people were human.

All you need is a talent for spotting the idiocies now built into the system. But you'll have to give up being an administrator who loves to run others and become a manager who carries water for his people so they can get on with the job. And you'll have to keep a suspicious eye on the phonies who cater to your uncertainties or feed your trembling ego on press releases, office perquisites, and optimistic financial reports. You'll have to give substance to such tired rituals as the office party. And you'll certainly have to recognize, once you get a hunk of your company's stock, that you aren't the last man who might enjoy the benefits of shareholding. These elegant simplicities require a sense of justice that won't be easy to hang on to.

I wrote this book when I realized how friends in one small company were being diverted by the glitter of the monster models: if *Time Inc. puts its executives in fancy offices, that must be the way to be big.* Model-watching has both a crude and subtle influence upon people at every level in every kind of work. To help start a counter-movement in that company, I Xeroxed a draft of this book and left a copy on each desk before anybody got to work.

If you master each section and focus your imagination

on helping your employees get everything they can deserve, you and they will probably come back to life and get rich.

Don't blame me if that doesn't solve any of your problems

CONTENTS

15 CONTENTS

A ADVERTISING

Fire the whole advertising department and your old agency. Then go get the best new agency you can. And concentrate your efforts on making it fun for them to create candid, effective advertising for you. Unless you've just done this, the odds favor that you have a bunch of bright people working at cross purposes to produce — at best — mediocre ads. We started at Avis by asking a few people for a list of the hottest agencies. Then we called on the creative heads of those agencies and tried to interest them in the rent a car business. Ultimately we stumbled on the right question: "How do we get five million dollars of advertising for one million dollars?" (our competition has five dollars for each dollar we have, and yet we have to pay the same price for cars, insurance, rent, gas, oil and people).

Finally, Bill Bernbach heard the question and answered: "If you want five times the impact, give us ninety days to learn enough about your business to apply our skills, and then run every ad we write where we tell you to run it. Our people work to see how effective their ideas are. But most clients put our ads through a succession of Assistant

V.P.'s and V.P.'s of advertising, marketing, and legal until we hardly recognize the remnants. If you promise to run them just as we write them, you'll have every art director and copywriter in my shop moonlighting on your account."

We shook hands on it.*

Ninety days later, Bill Bernbach came out to show Avis his recommended ads. He said he was sorry but the only honest things they could say were that the company was second largest and that the people were trying harder. Bernbach said his own research department had advised against the ads, that he didn't like them very much himself—but it was all they had so he was recommending them. We didn't like them much at Avis either, but we had agreed to run whatever Bill recommended.

The rest is history. Our internal sales growth rate increased from 10 per cent to 35 per cent in the next couple of years.

Moral: **Don't hire a master to paint you a masterpiece and then assign a roomful of schoolboy-artists to look over his shoulders and suggest improvements.**

---

* To keep people at Avis and at Doyle Dane Bernbach from violating Bernbach's vision of the ideal account. I wrote "The Avis Rent A Car Advertising Philosophy," had it framed, and hung it in everyone's office (at both client and agency). It reads :

ALPHABETICAL ORDER

Make sure that whoever types your infrequent memos
(*see* Memorandum, the Last) uses alphabetical order.
Otherwise some of your people will go through
Freudian agonies as their names rise and fall on the
addressee list and they appear to rise and fall in your
favor.

AVIS RENT A CAR
ADVERTISING PHILOSOPHY

1. Avis will never know as much about advertising as DDB, and DDB will never know as much about the rent a car business as Avis.
2. The purpose of the advertising is to persuade the frequent business renter (whether on a business trip, a vacation trip, or renting an extra car at home) to try Avis.
3. A serious attempt will be made to create advertising with five times the effectiveness (see #2 above) of the competition's advertising.
4. To this end, Avis will approve or disapprove, not try to improve, ads which are submitted. Any changes suggested by Avis must be grounded on a material operating defect (a wrong uniform for example).
5. To this end, DDB will only submit for approval those ads which they as an agency recommend. They will not "see what Avis thinks of that one."
6. Media selection should be the primary responsibility of DDB. However, DDB is expected to take the initiative to get guidance from Avis in weighting of markets or special situations, particularly in those areas where cold numbers do not indicate the real picture. Media judgments are open to discussion. The conviction should prevail. Compromises should be avoided.

ASSISTANTS-TO
AND MAKE-WORKING

The only people who thoroughly enjoy being assistants-to are vampires. The assistant-to operates in a very different way from an assistant. The regular line assistant has the authority of his boss when his boss is away and can therefore make the tactical day-to-day decisions that permit the surrounding areas of the company to keep functioning.

The differences can be seen by drawing three kinds of organizations:

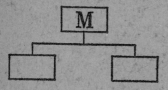

1. Best organization.

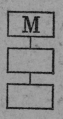

2. Twenty-five per cent less effective. Each level of management lowers communication effectiveness within the organization by about 25 per cent.

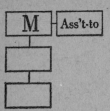

3. The absolute worst. Usually the sign of a weak, ineffective manager.

The assistant-to recommends itself to the weak or lazy manager as a crutch. It helps him where he shouldn't and can't be helped—head-to-head contact with his people. A good man deserves direct confrontation with his boss— especially when they're not in full accord. If all he gets is visits and memos from an assistant-to, he's entitled to blow his stack and go find a smarter boss somewhere.

There are some intelligent people doing assistant-to work: getting between the boss and the people who report to him, usurping power, crossing wires, and draining the organization's strength and zeal. You can't really blame the assistant-to. He wound up there because the boss got overworked and then followed his instincts. Instead of giving pieces of his job to other line officers, or carving out a whole job and giving it to someone to run with, he hired an assistant-to, and immediately became much less effective than he was when he was just overworked.

Another problem. You can't tell an assistant-to by his title. Some are called V.P. or Senior V.P. or Executive V.P. or even Chairman of the Executive Committee. But you can always tell one by the way he operates. He moves back and forth between the boss and his people with oral or written messages on real or apparent problems— overlapping and duplicating efforts and make-working.

In my book anyone who has an assistant-to should be fined a hundred dollars a day until he eliminates the position.

B 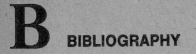BIBLIOGRAPHY

By far the best two books I've ever read on the subject of getting things done through organizations are: *Managing for Results* by Peter F. Drucker, New York, Harper & Row, 1964, and London, Pan Books: and *The Human Side of Enterprise* by Douglas McGregor New York, McGraw-Hill, 1960.

BIG WHEELS
IN LITTLE COMPANIES

Small companies can hire big-company retirees when the
man is going to exercise specific skills. It doesn't matter
how big or little the company is. But it won't work with
generalists. Small companies must be Spartan to survive.
Big companies are small companies that succeeded. Most
of them have become epicurean institutions. And their
fat cats have developed a lot of bad habits.

I know one small outfit that hired a big-company generalist
as president when he retired. His first four acts were:

1. Put his son-in-law on the payroll as his assistant-to.
2. Order a private bathroom built next to his office.
3. Order a reserved parking space in front of the building.
4. Take his wife on a three-month trip around the world.

It almost killed the little company.

BOSS, HOW TO RETIRE THE

The most successful retirement I ever saw was that of
Walter L. Jacobs, founder of the rent a car industry and
president of Hertz. For five years Walter kept telling
everybody he was going to go. He turned authority and
responsibility over to his younger people and built up
personal banking and real estate interests in his selected
retirement locale—to soak up the energy that might otherwise tempt him to be a pest. When Walter retired neither
he nor anyone else went into shock. And the company
made new records.

Please don't underestimate the destructive potential of the
retired chief executive who remains on the premises as a
"consultant" or Chairman of the Finance Committee. If
you are stuck with a predecessor who has contractual
rights to an office and a secretary, insist that he be
physically located somewhere else. You can afford to rent
him a handsome suite. Otherwise neither you, nor he,
nor anyone else will know who's in charge.

BUDGETS

. . . must not be prepared on high and cast as pearls before swine. They must be prepared by the operating divisions.

Since a division must believe in the budget as its own plan for operations, management cannot juggle figures just because it likes to. Any changes must be sold to the division or the whole process is a sham.

Statements comparing budget to actual should be written not in the usual terms of higher (lower) but in plain English of better (or worse) than predicted by the budget. This eliminates the mental gear changes between income items (where parens are bad) and expense items (where parens are good). This way *all* parens become bad, and reports can be understood faster.

Most lenders, directors, and owners look at the monthly report to see if you made your budget. If you did, into the file with it. If you didn't, the report goes to an uninformed nitpicker who dreams up a lot of stupid questions. To save yourself this agony, put some arbitrary safety factor into the top statements that go outside the company. You haven't distorted the figures by which you and your managers are trying to measure trends, but you have

something you can use to offset unforeseen setbacks without missing the budget as far as your investor/lenders
are concerned.

C CALL YOURSELF UP

When you're off on a business trip or a vacation, pretend you're a customer. Telephone some part of your organization and ask for help. You'll run into some real horror shows. Don't blow up and ask for name, rank, and serial number—you're trying to correct, not punish. If it happens on a call to the Dubuque office, just suggest to the manager (through channels, dummy) that he make a few test calls himself.

Then try calling yourself up and see what indignities you've built into your own defenses.

CHAIRMAN OF THE EXECUTIVE COMMITTEE

Most companies are doing it all wrong. They're wasting this title (and others like Vice-Chairman or Chairman of the Finance Committee) on retired brass. Just because no one has the guts to tell old Mr. Leatherhead (our founder) that now's the time for him to go take those scuba lessons he always wanted.

These titles can be very useful.

A certain national institute was created recently. It had a young director with a good deal of experience in the field, but not much experience in managing an organization. He had his objectives clearly thought out and budgets prepared showing how and where he hoped to reach them, and what it would mean to the industry. But it was already clear that one of his problems was going to be visits and phone calls from international visiting firemen and from people in the industry wanting to talk to the boss.

He had no room in his budget for an assistant and besides people won't be pushed off on an assistant. He *did* have a substantial expense account for entertainment. So he called up an old friend who was retired and said, "I can't pay you a salary, but if you'll come in and take all

these phone calls and lunches and dinners off my back,
I'll make you Chairman of the Executive Committee. You
can have some fun and meet some interesting people. And
I can spend full time getting the institute going."

The key is the title. Nobody knows what it means. Bob
Woodruff ran the Coca-Cola Company as Chairman of the
Executive Committee. It can mean much or nothing. But
nobody ever gets mad when the boss says, "Let me switch
you to the Chairman of our Executive Committee—this is
the kind of thing he takes charge of."

In a business context, I've seen this work in an area like
customer complaints. People who write or call with
complaints want someone to listen, sympathize, apologize,
and, if indicated, correct the matter. And the higher up
their complaint is handled the quicker their fire goes out.
But companies still insist on having these complaints
handled by "customer-service departments" or "complaint departments" or "adjustment departments". If I'm
switched to one of those, I'm twice as mad as when I
called. But I'm docile as a lamb if I hear, "Let me switch
you to the Chairman of the Executive Committee. One of
his people will take care of you. He likes to hear about
all the complaints." I could be talking to the same clerk
in the same department (except he is now speaking for
the Chairman of the Executive Committee). And the
letter of apology on that glorious letterhead not only rubs
out my grievance, but retains me as customer and gives

me something to brag about to your other prospects.*
The Russians have the best system. The real head of
their typical embassy is a third assistant attaché, who is
completely free of social obligations and can therefore
devote himself fully to running the operation, while the
French, British, German and American ambassadors
exhaust themselves on the cocktail- and dinner-party
circuit.

* If you are worried about the quality of the letters, ask them to
send you blind copies — but not hold up the letters for your reaction.
You must be careful not to nitpick. If the letters are substandard,
rewrite the worst ones and keep your drafts until you have a dozen
or so. Then go in and discuss yours compared with theirs. They'll
appreciate the help and their letters will improve.

COMPROMISE
AND KING SOLOMON

Compromise is usually bad. It should be a last resort. If two departments or divisions have a problem they can't solve and it comes up to you, listen to both sides and then, unlike Solomon, pick one or the other. This places solid accountability on the winner to make it work.

Condition your people to avoid compromise. Teach them to win some battles, lose others gracefully. Work on the people who try to win them all. For the sake of the organization, others must have a fair share of victories.

When you give in, give in all the way. And when you win, try to win all the way so the responsibility to make it work rests squarely on you.

COMPUTERS
AND THEIR PRIESTS

First get it through your head that computers are big,
expensive, fast, dumb adding-machine-typewriters. Then
realize that most of the computer technicians that you're
likely to meet or hire are complicators, not simplifiers.
They're trying to make it look tough. Not easy. They're
building a mystique, a priesthood, their own mumbo-
jumbo ritual to keep you from knowing what they—and
you—are doing.

Here are some rules of thumb:

1. *At this state of the art, keep decisions on computers at
   the highest level. Make sure the climate is ruthlessly
   hard-nosed about the practicality of every system,
   every program, and every report.* "What are you going
   to do with that report?" "What would you do if you
   didn't have it?" *Otherwise your programmers will be
   writing their doctoral papers on your machines, and
   your managers will be drowning in ho-hum reports
   they've been conned into asking for and are ashamed
   to admit are of no value.*
2. *Make sure your present report system is reasonably
   clean and effective before you automate. Otherwise
   your new computer will just speed up the mess.*

3. *Rather than build your own EDP staff, hire a small, independent software company to come in, plan your computer system, and then get out. Make sure they plan every detail in advance and let them know you expect them to meet every dollar and time target. Systems are like roads. Very expensive. And no good building them up until you know exactly where they're going to wind up.*

4. *Before you hire a computer specialist, make it a condition that he spend some time in the factory and then sell your shoes to the customers. A month the first year, two weeks a year thereafter. This indignity* will separate those who want to use their skills to help your company from those who just want to build their own know-how on your payroll.*

5. *No matter what the experts say, never, never, automate a manual faction without a long enough period of dual operation. When in doubt discontinue the automation. And don't stop the manual system until the non-experts in the organization think that automation is working. I've never known a company seriously injured by automating too slowly but there are some classic cases of companies bankrupted by computerizing prematurely.*

---

* Everybody including the chief executive had to go through the Avis rental-agent training school. I once saw the Ph.D. who was responsible for all Avis systems panic and run from an O'Hare rental counter at the approach of his first real customer.

CONFERENCE BOARD:
WHAT OTHERS DID, DON'T

The National Industrial Conference Board is a
sophisticated center of research on yesterday. A nonprofit
organization, it is paid by its member business organizations according to size or profit. Any conventional
company can join.

NICB publishes all sorts of data about corporate
practices. I've found it a valuable source for ideas —
on what *not* to do.* When the vast majority of big
companies are in agreement on some practice or policy,
you can be fairly certain that it's out of date. Ask
yourself: "What's the opposite of this conventional
wisdom?" And then work back to what makes sense.

---

* A few titles from the 1969 index of NICB publications will give you
the idea :
a) "The Board Chairman—Positions and duties." A job description
is included. From this came the conviction that job descriptions are
absurd for jobs above $150 a week.
b) "Human Relations—Personnel directors' responsibility for employee motivation . . . 'Employee Motivation—What role for personnel?' " From this came the conviction that we don't need a
personnel department at all.

CONFLICT WITHIN THE ORGANIZATION

. . . a sign of a healthy organization—up to a point. A good manager doesn't try to eliminate conflict; he tries to keep it from wasting the energies of his people (*see* Compromise and King Solomon; Memorandum, the Last; Salary Review: Annual Encounter Group).

Conviction is a flame that must burn itself out—in trying an idea or fighting for a chance to try it. If bottled up inside, it will eat a man's heart away.

If you're the boss and your people fight you openly when they think you're wrong—that's healthy. If your men fight each other openly in your presence for what they believe in—that's healthy. But keep all the conflict eyeball to eyeball (*see* Memorandum, the Last).

c) "Committees—Use of committees in developing policies." From this came the conviction that you should liquidate all permanent committees.
d) "Executives—Fringe benefits. Special fringe benefits, such as country-club memberships and chauffeurs to attract and hold top executives." From this came the conviction that you shouldn't have any of this nonsense paid for by the company.

CONTACTS

A lesson very few have learned: if you want to approach
the head of XYZ Corporation, call him cold. Tell him
who you are and why you want to talk to him. A direct
and uncomplicated relationship will follow.

The common mistake is to look for a mutual friend —
or a friend's friend on his board, in his bank or
investment bank or law firm — to introduce you. This
starts all sorts of side vibrations and usually results in a
half-assed prologue by the intermediary, who is apt to
grind both edges of his own axe.

CONTROLLERS
AND ACCOUNTING

No accounting system is very good, and all of them are infinitely variable. What the controller should do is insist that management pick one system and then not let them change it. He must be very strong on this point. Otherwise the management will fall or leap into the trap of inconsistency. The easiest way to do a snow job on investors (or on yourself) is to change one factor in the accounting each month. Then you can say, "It's not comparable with last month or last year. And we can't really draw any conclusion from the figures."

In a profit squeeze, management will come up with very creative reasons for changing the accounting system. They may even call on the outside accountants for support: "Isn't this better?" "Yes, that's better." But the point is: Is it a change? If it is, don't let them make it. This rule does not apply to the *very* occasional changes *originated* by the controller to show a more honest picture.

The controller will frequently be asked for figures in a hurry. He must never lose his head—that's what managements do, not controllers. If he does prepare a hurried report, he should label it for what it is: "Prepared under pressure and not understood."

The point is that if management wants to destroy its credibility with investors and with itself by preparing quickie projections and fearless forecasts, let it do so. But any report signed by the controller should be understood and believed honest (conservative) by the controller before he releases it. The controller's job is to see that all future surprises are pleasant.

The controller should never lose sight of his function: to provide an honest notation system by which managers can take responsible action towards their chosen goals and measure their progress. Honest reports are antibureaucratic; they give everybody a common starting-point from which to argue and make decisions.

A strategy meeting is apt to generate more heat than light unless everybody is talking from a common set of numbers.

The controller must not prepare or perpetrate reports for the Smithsonian archives. If his reports aren't useful to the line managers, they shouldn't be prepared.

From management's side, the important thing about getting the most out of the controller is to tell him about plans enough in advance so he can provide his input. Controllers are professionals. They don't gossip. Treat them as full members of the inner council. Save lots of agony by letting the controller have a good look at new ideas before they're implemented. If controllers are elected to insidership, they'll be valuable. If they're treated like plumber's helpers, they'll get their kicks making ends instead of means out of their reports and their systems — and you can't blame them. Yes, Virginia, accountants *are* people.

There abideth accuracy, timeliness, understanding, and unflappability in the controller's office — and the greatest of these is all four of them.

CONVICTION VS. EGO

Things get done in our society because of a man or woman with conviction.

Bill Bernbach, when he was building the most exciting advertising agency of his time, had a round conference table in his office. He tried the customary rectangular one, but, as he said, "The junior men always sat at the foot and I sat at the head, and I learned that the light of conviction is often in the eyes of the junior men. With a round table, I was closer to them and less likely to miss it."

At the other extreme the economy is crowded with giant institutions—scientific, religious, educational, or artistic—that are not centers of conviction but monuments to an ego. There is probably one in your neighborhood. I have several in mind. Lots of money goes into them. Lots of good people work there. No results.

Before you commit yourself to a new effort, it's worth asking yourself a couple of questions: "Are we really trying to do something worthwhile here?" "Or are we just building another monument to some diseased ego?"

D DECISIONS

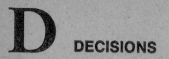

All decisions should be made as low as possible in the organization. The Charge of the Light Brigade was ordered by an officer who wasn't there looking at the territory.

There are two kinds of decisions: those that are expensive to change and those that are not.

A decision to build the Edsel or Mustang (or locate your new factory in Orlando or Yakima) shouldn't be made hastily; nor without plenty of inputs from operating people and specialists.

But the common or garden-variety decision—like when to have the cafeteria open for lunch or what brand of pencil to buy—should be made *fast*. No point in taking three weeks to make a decision that can be made in three seconds—and corrected inexpensively later if wrong. The whole organization may be out of business while you oscillate between baby-blue or buffalo-brown coffee cups.

DELEGATION OF AUTHORITY

Many give lip service, but few delegate authority *in important matters*. And that means all they delegate is dog-work. A real leader does as much dog-work for his people as he can: he can do it, or see a way to do without it, ten times as fast. And he delegates as many important matters as he can because that creates a climate in which people grow.

Example:
An important contract with a supplier comes up for renewal: There is your present supplier and a major competitor. How many managers would delegate that decision? You're right: none. But you should. Here's one way:

1. *Find the man in your organization to whom a good contract will mean the most. (Can't be more than two levels below you—there's that bloody organization chart getting in the way.)*
2. *Take the pains to write out on one sheet of paper the optimum and the minimum that you expect from each area of the contract.*
3. *Give your organization (including John—the man you've picked to negotiate) a couple of days to discuss your outline, edit, subtract, delete, add, and modify. Then rewrite it, call John into the office (with his boss*

*if there is one between him and you—I assume he's
in favor of this or forget it).*

4. *With John on an extension you phone the top man
involved at each supplier, and after the amenities, you
say: "This is John. I've asked him to negotiate this
contract. Whatever he recommends, we'll do. There is
no appeal over his head. I want a signed contract
within thirty days."*

Now, I know that ninety-nine out of a hundred managers
won't take this risk. But is it a risk? John is closer to the
point of use. He will be most affected by a bad contract.
He knows how much the company gains or loses by a
concession in each area (and they know he does). And
he'll spend full time on it for the next thirty days. Would
you? I maintain the company will get a more favorable
contract every time.

Note that you've given maximum authority and accountability to John. And you've been fair to (and put great
pressure on) your suppliers by telling them the rules
in advance.

Another example: Take two kinds of executives. Fred
operates in the traditional way with his legal department.
Some contracts he reads carefully and blue-pencils.
Others he returns with a question (implying he has read
carefully). Some he just signs. There is a feeling among
his lawyers that Fred reviews the documents anyway, so
occasionally they get sent upstairs right from the
typewriter.

Bill's approach is different. He has said to his general
counsel: "I don't want to read any legal documents
covering transactions I've approved. If I have to sign
them, then you initial them for legal aspects, and get the
affected division or department head to initial for
operating aspects. But remember, if you send it in with
those two sets of initials, I'll sign it without reading it."

It seems to me Bill's way places the accountability where
it belongs and protects the shareholders better without
increasing the legal expenses. It also eliminates a lot of
bulky papers that should never get in the chief executive's
briefcase anyway.

DIRECTORS, BOARD OF:
THE BACK-SEAT DRIVERS

The huge, successful company is a dinosaur, but it has
one decisive advantage over the middle-size outfit that's
trying to grow public; also over the established company
that's in trouble enough to be ready for change. The
advantage: most big companies have turned their boards
of directors into non-boards. The chief executive has put
his back-seat drivers to sleep.

This achievement has to be understood to be admired. In
the years that I've spent on various boards I've never
heard a single suggestion from a director (made *as* a
director *at* a board meeting) that produced any result
at all.

While ostensibly the seat of all power and responsibility,
directors are usually the friends of the chief executive
put there to keep him safely in office. They meet once a
month, gaze at the financial window dressing (never at
the operating figures by which managers run the
business), listen to the chief and his team talk superficially
about the state of the operation, ask a couple of
dutiful questions, make token suggestions (courteously
recorded and subsequently ignored), and adjourn until
next month.

Over their doodles around the table, alert directors spend their time in silent worry about their personal obligations and liabilities in a business they can't know enough about to understand. The danger is that their consciences, or fears, may inspire them now and then to dabble, all in the name of responsibility.

Two simple tactics have been devised and time-tested in large organizations to head off this threat.

First, make sure that the board is composed partly of outsiders and partly of officers. Since all the important questions relate to the performance of key men and their divisions, no important questions will be asked. To do so would be a breach of etiquette, an insult to somebody at the table. Nor will any officer-director with an instinct for self-preservation (and a modicum of respect for the ignorance of the outside directors) ever bring a new or controversial idea before the board.

Second, be sure to serve cocktails and a heavy lunch before the meeting. At least one of the older directors will fall asleep (literally) at the meeting and the consequent embarrassment will make everyone eager to get the whole mess over as soon as possible. Caution: let sleeping directors lie. If one ever finds out that you rely on his somnolence, he will come to life with fierce and angry energy.

Unfortunately, smaller/newer companies often have directors who are investors or lenders able to exert the power of ownership. These directors are generally disastrous in their effect upon young managements. If not firmly under the thumb of the chief executive, they indulge a nervous impulse: they keep pulling up the flowers to see how the roots are growing.

Directors and the like (*see* Management and "Top" Management) spend very little time studying and worrying about your company. Result: they know far less than you give them credit for. What they know you can get best by a phone call. It is dangerous to take their formal advice seriously, or be too earnest about their casual questions. If they can ask important questions that the chief executive hasn't already thought of, he ought to be replaced.

Directors have one function, other than declaring dividends, which is theirs to perform: they can and must judge the chief executive officer, and throw him out when the time comes.* So the manager of a small/new company must come to these terms: he must make it clear from the outset that he accepts without question the right of the directors to assemble whenever they want and decide to replace him. Having in effect signed a resignation datable at their pleasure, he must meet with them quarterly for a whole day and report to them on the state and trend of the business. These four meetings and the monthly statements should enable the directors to judge him and fulfill their one significant function when the time comes.

* Since this task is painful, it is rarely performed even when all the directors know it is long overdue.

Replacements for retiring directors should be other chief executives in completely unrelated businesses or experts active in related fields of knowledge. But suppliers of goods and services—like lawyers, accountants, bankers and investment bankers—should be kept off the board if at all possible. Give one of these a seat, and you shut off healthy competition from his profession to serve your company.

DISOBEDIENCE
AND ITS NECESSITY

A commander in chief [manager] cannot take as an excuse for his mistakes in warfare [business] an order given by his minister [boss] or his sovereign [boss's boss], when the person giving the order is absent from the field of operations and is imperfectly aware or wholly unaware of the latest state of affairs. It follows that any commander in chief [manager] who undertakes to carry out a plan which he considers defective is at fault; he must put forward his reasons, insist on the plan being changed and finally tender his resignation rather than be the instrument of his army's [organization's] downfall.

—NAPOLEON, Military Maxims and Thoughts

E EJACULATION, PREMATURE

If you discovered how to eliminate air pollution for $1.50 per state, the worst way to accomplish it would be to announce your discovery. You'd be amazed at how many people would oppose your scheme. The best way, if you could stay alive and out of jail, would be just to start eliminating it, state by state.

To get something done involving several departments, divisions or organizations, keep quiet about it. Get the available facts, marshal your allies, think through the opponents' defenses, and then go.

A premature announcement of what you're *going* to do unsettles potential supporters, gives opponents time to construct real and imaginary defenses, and tends to ensure failure.

It's a poor bureaucrat who can't stall a good idea until even its sponsor is relieved to see it dead and officially buried.

EMPLOYMENT CONTRACTS
AND WHY NOT

To the company they say, "We've got him locked in, so we don't have to worry about him or listen to him as much as if we didn't."

To the individual they say, "Here's a date when your loyalty expires. Start thinking well in advance on what terms you'll renew."

Without employment contracts, the company must keep the climate challenging and invigorating and the rewards commensurate with the performance. Contracts in my opinion usually lose the men they are designed to hold. And keep those who have no other basis for staying. At the root of the disaster in American education today is the tenure system—whether of those non-teaching professors at Berkeley or of Al Shanker's lard-assed civil servants in Brooklyn. And don't think the kids don't know it.

EPAULETS FOR
THE CHIEF EXECUTIVE

With any encouragement some people in your company
will spend full time getting the chief executive decorated
by foreign governments. Or putting his picture in the
papers, getting him made man-of-the-year by the
American Pizza Association, or press-released by that
new adventure in egomania, the American Academy of
Achievement. A good chief executive will knock off all
this nonsense. A weak one will accept the kudos because
his indifferent performance as chief executive creates in
him a real need for ego massage. Watch for the signs.
Then you'll know what kind of chief executive you
have—or are.

EXCELLENCE: OR,
WHAT THE HELL ARE
YOU DOING HERE?

If you can't do it excellently, don't do it at all.
Because if it's not excellent it won't be profitable or fun,
and if you're not in business for fun or profit, what the
hell are you doing here?

EXCUSES

When you get right down to it, one of the most important
tasks of a manager is to eliminate his people's excuses
for failure. But if you're a paper manager, hiding in
your office, they may not tell you about the problems only
you can solve. So get out and ask them if there's anything
you can do to help. Pretty soon they're standing right out
there in the open with nobody but themselves to blame.
Then they get to work, then they turn on to success, and
then they have the strength of ten.

EXPENSE ACCOUNTS:
THEORY X DISEASE

Like everything else you do—keep your expense account honest. Even if others are cheating openly. Not because you might get caught, but because honesty has to start somewhere. The people who are buying clothes or having their shirts laundered on their expense accounts are getting their fun that way because they're in a Theory X (*see* People) environment and can't get healthy kicks during office hours.

The typical response of a Theory X company to this game is to hire more people to write regulations and check the resulting paperwork. This costs more than the cheating, which, of course, doesn't stop—it just gets more inventive.

The real solution: repeal the regulations, fire the checkers, and start to build a Theory Y company (*see* People).

F FAIRNESS, JUSTICE, AND OTHER ODDITIES

Fairness, justice, or whatever you call it — it's essential and most companies don't have it. Everybody must be judged on his performance, not on his looks or his manners or his personality or who he knows or is related to.

Performances are distributed along the normal bell-shaped curve; a few outstanding ones at one end, the vast majority of satisfactory ones in the middle, and a few undeniably lousies at the other end.

Rewarding outstanding performances is important. Much more neglected is the equally important need to make sure that the underachievers *don't* get rewarded. This is more painful, so it doesn't get done very often.

You never know who is reacting to what part of your effort to be fair. Some may flee the stick and some are drawn to the carrot. It's your job to create a system that's fair.* And that's not easy. Injustice is built into our society and even into our instincts. To paraphrase Dwight Morrow, the world seems to be divided into those who produce the results and those who get the credit.

* For some thoughts on keeping the President's salary fair, *see* President's Salary (Is He Really Worth $250,000?).

FAMILY BAGGAGE

The worst wives (from the standpoint of the effect on
their husbands) in my experience are the overly
ambitious ones. They seem to be constantly after their
husbands to make more money. They don't understand
that money, like prestige, if sought directly, is almost
never gained. It must come as a byproduct of some
worthwhile objective or result which is sought and
achieved for its own sake.

FIRING PEOPLE

Firing people is unpleasant but it really has to be done occasionally. It's a neglected art in most organizations. If a guy isn't producing after a year (two at most), admit that you were wrong about him. Keeping him is unfair to other people who must make up for his failure and untangle his mess. And it's unfair to him. He might do well in another company or industry.

Managers often duck this duty because it's unpleasant. But purging the bad performers is as good a tonic for the organization as giving sizable rewards to the star performers. Under profit sharing, you penalize the able by holding on to the inept.

Keep in mind that first impressions of performance are often wrong. There are slow starters who become stars, and flashes in the pan who sputter out.

Don't be needlessly cruel in firing someone. Figure out a reason that is true but enables him to preserve his ego. It is usually true that his combination of skills is not what's needed, or that the job is being restructured. If you don't feel compelled to destroy his self-regard, he can move on quickly without scars.

A good way to tell a line man from a staff man is to find out how many people he has personally fired. If only one or two, he may well be a staff man by nature. If put in a line position he may agonize for days over getting rid of some bad performer. He may hang on to one who clearly can't make it, or rig a transfer that puts a wounded blood-hungry tiger into another part of the company. A good line man backs his gut feeling that Charlie is wrong for the job, fires him, and suffers a sleepless night or two. But the whole organization gets reinforced if he's right.

If you've inherited (or built) an office that needs a real house cleaning, the only sure cure is move the whole thing out of town, leaving the dead wood behind. One of my friends has done it four times with different companies. The results are always the same:

1. *The good ones are confident of their futures and go with you.*
2. *The people with dubious futures (and their wives) don't have to face the fact that they've been fired. "The company left town," they say. They get job offers, quickly, usually from your competitors who think they're conducting a raid.*
3. *The new people at Destiny City are better than the ones you left behind and they're infused with enthusiasm because they've been exposed only to your best people.*

G GEOGRAPHY, RESPECT FOR

If your business is in Cleveland, start or acquire an operation in Santa Barbara at your peril. Absentee management is fatal.

And the disaster potential is equal to the square of the distance — measured in hours — between your home base and the new plant. No matter how determined you are to visit it frequently, you'll discover that your capacity to find last-minute reasons not to go is unlimited.

If the new operation is in Europe or the Far East, the problems increase by cube functions. It is twenty-seven times harder to cope with an operation in Hong Kong tha in Duluth.

GIFTS FROM SUPPLIERS

Right after Thanksgiving, put out the following memo in your own language and style:

There is nothing wrong with having personal friendships with representatives of those companies with whom we do business. However, this cannot be permitted to extend to the giving or receiving of gifts.

It is therefore against our policy for any employee to accept from any company or representative of a supplier company with whom we do or may do business any gifts of value, including cash, merchandise, gift certificates, weekend or vacation trips. This means, of course, returning any such gifts which may be delivered to your home or office.

Please see that the people within your area of responsibility are aware of this policy immediately.

Maybe people can keep two bottles of whisky or the equivalent. Anything more than that should be returned with thanks for the thought.

You can avoid embarrassing your friend the supplier by letting him read the memo. Swapping gifts is an insult to him and to you. It implies (1) that he's got to con you because he's cheating your company, and (2) that you're ready to accept the favor because you could make a better deal if you tried.

GOING A LITTLE BIT PUBLIC

Small privately-owned businesses are tempted in hot stock markets to register with the SEC and sell a little stock.

Result One: The stock is quoted.

Result Two: The few employees and friends who own registered stock sell or buy a few shares a week and the stock moves!

Result Three: The company doesn't sell the 15-million-dollar convertible issue that is needed for solid expansion (*"Gee, the stock is selling at 14 dollars a share—the company is worth 60 million dollars—why should we give away 40 per cent of it for 15 million dollars"*). Or management is afraid to shut down the perennial loss division (*"It might hurt the price of the stock"*).

The valuation based on the tiny amount of stock traded is purely fictitious. But the mistakes made because of this purely paper value are costly. Sometimes deadly.

When André Meyer, senior partner of Lazard Frères, and I were talking about whether or not I'd run Avis for him, one of my requests (to which he readily agreed) was that neither of us would mention the price of the stock for two years. Most investment bankers, whose idea of a long-term investment is thirty-six hours, would never have agreed.

H HARVARD BUSINESS SCHOOL*

Don't hire Harvard Business School graduates.
This worthy enterprise confesses that it trains its students
for only three posts — executive vice-president, president,
and board chairman. The faculty does not blush when
HBS is called the West Point of capitalism.

By design, the "B-School' trains a senior officer class,
the non-playing Captains of Industry. People who, upon
graduation, are given a whirlwind tour of their chosen
company and then an office and a secretary and some
work to do while they wait for one of the top three slots
to open up.

This elite, in my opinion, is missing some pretty
fundamental requirements for success: humility; respect
for people on the firing line; deep understanding of the
nature of the business and the kind of people who can
enjoy themselves making it prosper; respect from way
down the line; a demonstrated record of guts, industry,
loyalty down, judgment, fairness, and honesty under
pressure.

* On page 372 of *The Age of Discontinuity*, Peter F. Drucker writes,
"The business schools in the U.S., set up less than a century ago, have
been preparing well-trained clerks. . . ." Peter, who is a good guy
and shouldn't be judged by his pupils, ought to know. He teaches at
NYU's business school.

I've already applied (no acknowledgment) for the job of guide to the Harvard Business School in 1995. By that time tourists will be wandering around it like Stonehenge, asking, "I wonder what they used to do here?"

HEADHUNTERS

Occasionally (rarely, I hope) you may have to disregard
the rule of 50 per cent (*see* Promotion, From Within) and
go outside to fill an opening.

If you use a headhunter, go to the trouble of writing out
your description of just the man you need (in your own
words, not job-description boiler-plate). When he sends in
a man for an interview, spend some time with him, even
if at first glance he's not what you're looking for. Then
call up your headhunter and tell him in some detail where
he's on target and where he's off. Do this after each
candidate. Pretty soon he'll zero in and start sending you
the kind of people you want to choose from.

HUBRIS, THE SIN OF

Managers tend to make their biggest mistakes in things they've previously done best. In business, as elsewhere, hubris is the unforgivable sin of acting cocky when things are going well. As the Greeks tiresomely told us, Hubris is followed inexorably and inevitably by Nemesis.

I INCENTIVE COMPENSATION AND PROFIT SHARING

Some of this may not be applicable to your business, but the philosophy is.

To be effective, an incentive-compensation system of profit sharing should include the following characteristics:

1. *It should be related as directly as possible to performance. Therefore, wherever a participant has primary responsibility for a profit centre his incentive compensation is directly related on a percentage basis to the profits of that center. Where his relationship is more remote, or where his judgments are of a staff type, evaluation is based on the judgment of his boss, but this is far less desirable.*

   ¶ *Spend company time and effort on the preparation of profit-and-loss statements for profit centers to enable as many people as practicable to be measured that way.*

   ¶ *Recognize that to have maximum effectiveness, profit-center-related bonuses must be computed in accordance with an accounting system which everyone understands and recognizes as fair. Therefore, all overheads should be brought down to the bottom line for bonus purposes on principles agreed to in advance. In order to avoid hours of hair-splitting, review the fairness every six months.*

   ¶ *It is most desirable that a man be able to measure himself as he goes forward through the year, since he spends more time with himself than his boss does.*

There his percentage of profits must be agreed to in advance.

¶ *For maximum effectiveness, no ceiling should be put on a profit-measured bonus merely because it has become substantial. On the other side of the same idea, don't let any paternalistic feeling ameliorate the situation of a manager whose business has turned bad and who, for the first time, may receive no bonus at all.*

2. *Employees who do not have sufficient funds to support their reasonable family needs are distracted from their efforts. Accordingly, attempt to have salary measure the job itself and provide enough money for reasonable living costs. Incentive compensation is to measure variations in performance.*

¶ *Within these principles, limit executive base salaries, particularly at the top. For companies up to $100 million sales or $10 million pre-tax net, the chief executive officer and his three or four key executives could all be within a $40,000-$50,000 top range with very little differential among them. It isn't necessary for the chief executive officer to be paid more than the other officers, any more than a professional football coach has to be paid more than the star players. It is, of course, necessary to have a chief executive officer.*

3. *Get your board of directors to establish in perpetuity (a moral binder) that 15 per cent of total pre-tax profit will be available for those eligible* for incentive compensation. The perpetuity is important. Otherwise the finks will try to reduce it when it becomes sizable.*

---

* Anyone who makes $15,000 *or* has other people reporting to him or her (supervisor of a key-punch shift for example might make $6000) could be eligible. In a very small organization (200 people or so) *everybody* should be eligible.

4. *Bonuses measured by profit centers are handled by formula. Changes in formula should be resisted.*
¶ *The determination of discretionary bonuses is critical and much more difficult.* Fairness and full disclosure are the two keys to making the system work. With this in mind:

(a) The performance of every employee with one year of service who is a candidate for bonus participation must be rated by his boss in one of three categories. It is extremly important to resist pressures to increase the number of categories because complication tends to defeat the effort to be fair. Any manager should be able to place each of his people easily in one of three categories, but it becomes much more difficult with five or six categories.

(b) Generally speaking, ratings fall in the classification of unsatisfactory, satisfactory, and outstanding. It is anticipated that approximately 10 per cent will be at each extreme. Any manager whose records show that he has no "unsatisfactory employees" may have an explanation to give to his boss. Similarly, one who has no "outstanding" employees over a lengthy period of time also has an explanation to give.

(c) Once the ratings have been made, the determination of bonuses is a purely mechanical job. Each unsatisfactory employee is given a rate of zero and will receive no bonus check. Each satisfactory employee will receive X per cent of his base salary. Each outstanding employee will receive $2X$ per cent. Extraordinary cases of multiple X per cent are also *added in.* The bonus pool produced by the 15 per cent of profits is then divided by total weighted salaries to produce the necessary computation of X per cent. An example of how this system works:*

Assume a company with 3,000 employees, $100 million of sales, $10 million of pre-tax, pre-incentive compensation earnings. Fifteen per cent of $10 million gives us a pool of $1.5 million available for incentive compensation. Assume 400 people are on incentives related to profit centers and their formula bonuses add up to $1 million. This leaves $500,000 for discretionary incentive-compensation payments. Assume 50 people are eligible (base salary of at least $15,000 or have other people reporting to them). Assume 4 are rated unsatisfactory (no bonus); 42 are rated satisfactory (X per cent of base salary), and 4 are rated outstanding (2X per cent of base pay). In this year assume no ratings higher than 2X.

DISCRETIONARY INCENTIVE COMPENSATION

Eligible Employees	Performanc Rating	Aggregate Base Salary	Incentive Compensation	Per cent of Base Salary
4	Unsatisfactory (0%)			
42	Satisfactory (X%)	$820,000	$426,000	52
4	Outstanding (2X%)	71,000	74,000	104
			$500,000	

X, in this case turns out to be 52 per cent.

* When you get all through with the 0, X, and 2X ratings, you ask, "Is there anyone with a 2X rating whose performance belongs in a class by itself?" If there is a 3X or 4X performance, it is generally acknowledged by acclamation.

There were 42 people with satisfactory ratings. Each will receive incentive compensation of 52 per cent of base salary. Four people were rated outstanding. Each will receive 104 per cent of base salary as incentive compensation. This is an important barrier to break through. It lets some people really taste blood.

¶ This system can be prostituted and become a means of overpaying fat cats at the top. The chief executive at Avis never received a higher rating than X per cent (satisfactory), and in one year received an unsatisfactory rating.*

(d) The message is as important as the medium, which is only money. Accordingly, bonus checks are NEVER DISTRIBUTED *by the chief executive officer, except to those reporting directly to him. Each bonus check is physically handed to an employee by his boss and is accompanied by a conversation (hopefully a dialogue and not a monologue) about the amount of the check (or absence of check) and the reasons for the evaluation. The most important conversations are with the employees who get no bonus checks because at that time one gets their undivided attention.*

Certain philosophical and psychological conditions follow from a system of the kind described above.

---

* I rated myself and then submitted the rating to the board of directors for approval. It was understood that they could lower but not raise the rating (*see* President's Salary [Is He Really Worth $250,000?]).

1. *In an ordinary economic sense, all management people are "partners" and, as such, have a major stake in one another's achievements.*
2. *There is a tough-minded attitude toward "carrying old Joe or his nephew" since everyone in the bonus system is paying for a share of old Joe or his nephew. People tend to be fairly outspoken where their pocketbooks are concerned.*

At the risk of repetition and to avoid misunderstandings, one might state the things which are *not* built into this compensation philosophy:

1. *No "thirteenth month" type of bonus or profit sharing by which every employee simply gets an extra pay period during the year, unrelated to his performance. Such an arrangement is worse than no incentive-compensation system because it misleads the directors and shareholders into believing that there is an incentive-compensation system when in fact there is none.*
2. *No incentive compensation is paid to an employee who does not otherwise merit it because "he is counting on it". Such a payment is always injurious to the organization and other employees, since it tends to reinforce the meritless one in the practices which justified an unsatisfactory rating.*
3. *No penalizing an employee—who has conducted himself well and shown tangible results—because of the failure of others either above him or elsewhere in the organization. Even during loss years when the*

company as a whole doesn't earn money, a few
outstanding managers will receive incentive
compensation or profit sharing based upon the results
of the area under their control.

4. No reducing the percentage participation of a manager
because his bonus is "getting too high," since such
fudging corrupts the entire system. Your stockholders
should yearn to have all your incentive-compensation
participants get four times their base pay in bonus.

5. There are no secrets. No private payroll, for example.
Since at least 15 per cent of your employees should
share in incentive compensation, it is very difficult to
keep them in the dark about any expenditure with
which they are unfairly burdened. Because all profit
centers carry full overhead, unnecessary overhead
items are known throughout the organization and
vocally resented. Accordingly, your executive people
should have none of the following items which would
reduce bonuses and cause resentment:

a) Directors' fees.
b) Executive Committee members' fees.
c) Company-paid luncheon, golf, country, or yacht
   clubs.
d) Executive aircraft.
e) Executive dining rooms or executive washroom.
f) Chauffeur-driven vehicles.
g) First-class air travel.
h) Company-paid travel expenses for family members.
i) Corporate philanthropy.

Your people should be encouraged to earn as much bonus as they can and then spend it on clubs, limousines, other corporate luxuries, or save it, or give it to charity. However, the choice should be theirs. Don't ask your people to subsidize the ego of fat cats at the top.

INDIRECTION:
DON'T NEGLECT IT

Whether you're working in the mailroom or running the whole show you'll be more effective if you vary your attack on your problems and opportunities. You'll also have more fun, and be less of a bore.

Know how something disappears if you stare at it long enough? And if everybody knows you're going to shout when you stand up, they'll turn off their receivers.

Work can be approached obliquely as well as directly. This is why people should be allowed to work out their own office hours and vacation patterns. Everybody will have a different system of building up a head of steam and then releasing it.

There is a time for engagement and a time for withdrawal. A time to walk around the job. A time to contemplate it—and a time to just laugh at it.

INSTITUTION,
ON NOT BECOMING AN

If you ever get a good Theory Y (*see* People)
organization going, the problem becomes how to keep it
that way.

One good plan is for the chief executive to insist that he
must personally use every form in the company before
it's installed. Like: requisition forms (for pencils, pads,
or air tickets), long-distance-telephone-call forms, or
personnel department forms. And his secretary can't fill
in the form for him.

If some psychiatrist in the personnel department invents
a new application form with a whole lot of questions like,
"How do you feel about your mother?", before it gets
used the chief executive has to fill it out . . . completely.
This will kill a lot of bad ideas early.

Related to this is a function that you might describe as
vice-president in charge of anti-bureaucratization. He
must have a loud voice, no fear, and a passionate hatred
for institutions and their practices. In addition to his
regular duties, it's his job to wander around the company
looking for new forms, new staff departments, and new
reports. Whenever he finds one that smells like

institutionalization, he screams "Horseshit!" at the top of his lungs. And keeps shouting until the new what-ever-it-is is killed.

Billy Graham has a man named Grady Wilson who yells "Horseshit" — however you say that in Baptist — at him whenever he takes himself too seriously. Perhaps that's one of the reasons the Graham organization has been so successful. I had a Chairman of the Executive Committee who used to blow a launch-caller at me.* Every chief executive should find someone to perform this function and then make sure he can be fired only for being too polite.

Since the leader must lead the battle against institutionalization, it's to the leader that you should look for early signs of losing the war. Is he getting confused about who's God? Polishing up the image instead of greasing the wheels? Preoccupied with the price of the stock? Listening to the public relations department? Short-tempered with honest criticism? Are people hesitating before they tell him? Is he avoiding risks? Playing it safe? Talking to only certain people? Invisible to the rank and file? Hasn't even met some of the new people? Saying the same old magic words but doing something different?

---

* I was also blessed with a colleague who would break me up every now and then with a top-secret beginning along these lines: "Dear Jefe de Oro: With regard to your latest pronunciamento, if you say so, it will be my hourly concern to make it so. But before I sally forth in service of this your latest cause, I must tell you with deep affection and respect that you're full of shit again . . . etc., etc." These epistles batted about .900.

Heartbreaking, isn't it? But he's probably had his five or six years and it's time for a new leader (*see* Wearing Out Your Welcome).

INVESTMENT BANKERS

Like other suppliers of services (CPA's, commercial bankers, cleaning ladies, and lawyers), investment bankers work better if they sense that you aren't married to them. You should try to keep at least one alternate waiting eagerly (or at least waiting) in the wings.

You do this by having a quarterly lunch or dinner with your alternate contact and by supplying him regularly with your monthly figures (if these people can't respect confidences, nobody can).

While working with your current lawyer or banker, you give him every opportunity to do a good job. You are entitled to expect excellence from him. If you don't get it over a period of time, you had best change firms. It is usually easier to change firms than to reshape a relationship that has gone sour (*see* Lawyers Can Be Liabilities).

INVESTORS:
KEEPING THEM INFORMED

They can be a nuisance when things are going well, but a
positive threat to the company's existence when things
have been going badly.

Here's how Lazard Frères handled the problem of
keeping themselves and other investors informed in one
case of a company they controlled. After the monthly
statements were released, a certain partner would phone
and say he was arriving at company headquarters the
following morning. On arrival, he would go into an office
by himself with a list of all division and department
heads who were expected to be at headquarters that day.
If some had planes to catch, that was noted on his list. He
called them in *one at a time* and asked them any questions
he wanted (they had all seen the same monthly statements
because they were circulated freely to them with the
caveat that they not be discussed outside the company).
If he asked a question that could be answered better by
someone else on the list, the questionee might ask to see
the list and then suggest: "Why not ask *him* that
question?" Or in some cases the questionee would have a
go at answering anyway. The chief executive was called
in for his half hour or so just like the others. At the end
of the day the Lazard partner left.

Within a week at the outside, a triple-spaced memo would arrive and be circulated rapidly to all the people who had been interviewed (or their deputies if they were out of town on that particular day). The report was corrected as to fact (not style) and then sent back to the Lazard partner the same day. He would have it typed up in final form and sent to the directors and investors.

Note that this process only took an hour or less a month from each manager at the company. Also, since everybody at the company who was interviewed read the whole memo, it was an excellent intra-company communications device.

Since the company had a chance to review and modify before it went to the investors, any promise or deadlines became doubly binding on the people who had made or set them.

Two things about this technique bear watching.

First, the same man always came every month. He never sent a substitute. So his knowledge and understanding of the company increased geometrically and his relationships with the individuals became easier and easier.

Second, he was an honest and fair reporter of what he found.

J JOB DESCRIPTIONS— STRAIT JACKETS

Great for key-punch operators and other jobs where the turnover is high and the work is largely repetitive.

Insane for jobs that pay $150 a week or more. Judgment jobs are constantly changing in nature and the good people should be allowed to use their jobs to see how good they are.

At best, a job description freezes the job as the writer understood it at a particular instant in the past. At worst, they're prepared by personnel people who can't write and don't understand the jobs. Then they're not only expensive to prepare and regularly revise, but they're important morale-sappers.

**KILLING THINGS,
V.P. IN CHARGE OF**

It's about eleven times as easy to start something as it is
to stop something. But ideas are good for a limited time
—not forever.*

If Curtis Publishing had had a good V.P. in charge of
killing things, the *Saturday Evening Post*, which was a
great idea for many years, would have been killed before
it ate up all those careers and all that capital.

The internal-combustion engine should long since have
been killed and replaced with some form of external-
combustion (pollutionless) engine.

General Foods, the AFL-CIO, the Bureau of the Budget,
and the Ford Foundation should make it a practice to wipe
out their worst product, service, or activity every so often.
And I don't mean cutting it back or remodeling it—I
mean right between the eyes.

And just to give us all a glimmer of light at the end of the
tunnel, how about making it a matter of law that the
federal government for the next hundred years will have
to kill two old activities for each new one they start?

* Dr. Robert Sobel, Associate Professor of History at Hofstra University, says that the British created a civil-service job in 1803 calling
for a man to stand on the Cliffs of Dover with a spyglass. He was
supposed to ring a bell if he saw Napoleon coming. The job was
abolished in 1945.

L LABOR UNIONS

. . . including civil service and the American Association
of University Professors, are a bloody nuisance.

Unionism, say the most idealistic leaders, has
deteriorated into a kind of industrial police force that
also sells insurance. The labor movement is now a
conservative bureaucracy that resists the creative change
of the good manager.

If you don't have them, the best way to avoid them is to
create a Theory Y environment (*see* People) where your
people have a chance to realize their potential (and get
recognition for their contribution) in helping the
company reach its objectives.

If you already have unions, then deal with them openly
and honestly. Abide by their rules. For example, be
meticulous about explaining every new benefit to the
delegate privately and well in advance. After all, you
want your people (union or not) to have the best deal you
can give them. Whether the union grabs the credit for
each item is completely immaterial. Don't sell your

people short — they know. And don't turn your people over to the union politician by refusing to initiate benefits on the theory that the union will demand more than you can offer anyway.

LAWYERS
CAN BE LIABILITIES

Getting good legal advice is a question of picking the right individual, not the right firm. Usually the best is a young lawyer on-the-make. Look for a partner, or an about-to-be partner, who hasn't yet brought in any new business.

A good lawyer will give you his home phone number, will travel on weekends and work weekends when it's needed, and will carry the corporate seal in his briefcase.

Beware of the lawyer who talks Middle English or statutory paragraph numbers. Though the common law did start before Chaucer, and though Congress does number sections of its output, you need a lawyer to answer questions, not to show off the glories of his trade.

Lawyers take to politics like bears to honey. Other things being equal, try to pick lawyers who are active in politics —particularly if you hire local lawyers in your regional operations (*see* Washington, D.C., Relations with). The best ones won't try or be able to "fix" things. But they're great antennae. Once you're identified as their client their friends in local and state governments will often talk to them before taking action that affects you.

LEADERSHIP

To lead the people, walk behind them.
                —LAO-TZU

True leadership must be for the benefit of the followers, not the enrichment of the leaders. In combat, officers eat last.

Most people in big companies today are administered, not led. They are treated as personnel, not people.

Something is happening to our country. We aren't producing leaders like we used to. A new chief executive officer today, exhausted by the climb to the peak, falls down on the mountaintop and goes to sleep.

Where are our corporate Ethan Allens and John Hancocks and Nathanael Greenes, to say nothing of our George Washingtons, Ben Franklins, and Thomas Jeffersons? If we had to get the modern equivalent of our Founding Fathers together today, the first thing they'd do is hire Cresap, McCormick, and Paget * to write the Constitution for them.

I'm afraid leadership is becoming a lost art:

"Most hierarchies are nowadays so cumbered with rules and traditions, and so bound in by public laws, that even

* Their initials, some say, stands for "Christ! more people!"

high employees do not have to lead anyone anywhere, in the sense of pointing out the direction and setting the pace. They simply follow precedents, obey regulations, and move at the head of the crowd. Such employees lead only in the sense that the carved wooden figurehead leads the ship."

How do you spot a leader? They come in all ages, shapes, sizes, and conditions. Some are poor administrators, some are not overly bright. One clue: since most people per se are mediocre, the true leader can be recognized because, somehow or other, his people consistently turn in superior performances.

"As for the best leaders, the people do not notice their existence. The next best, the people honor and praise. The next, the people fear; and the next, the people hate . . .

When the best leader's work is done the people say, 'We did it ourselves!'"†

* Peter and Hull: *The Peter Principle*. New York: Morrow; 1969.
† From Lao-tzu.

M MANAGEMENT AND "TOP" MANAGEMENT

"Top" management (the board of directors) is supposed to be a tree full of owls—hooting when management heads into the wrong part of the forest. I'm still unpersuaded they even know where the forest is (*see* Directors, Board of: the Back-Seat Drivers). "Top" management is free-floating and, like Gulliver's flying island Laputa, only occasionally in touch * with the real world of the company they're supposed to direct.

In the giant companies, it's an Elysian field † where you put your old pros (and a few legacies) to get them out of the way of the young Turks and let them figurehead annual charity drives. It's a pleasant vague world of ceremony and ritual built around the regular board and committee meetings. The chief executive, if he wants to be effective, spends a token ‡ amount of time eating lotus with these Mandarins.

When stripped of the pejorative "top," the word "management" to me means the chief executive officer and all others who have one or more people reporting to

---

* Ralph Cordiner, as a member of top management of G.E., really *didn't* know his people were conspiring to fix prices.
† Take the elevator to the thirty-fourth floor of the Time/Life Building in New York City. It's occasionally possible to walk all around it without seeing a living soul except for the two receptionists.
‡ Four board meetings a year are infinitely less wearing on your operating and accounting people than twelve.

them. Their jobs as managers are fundamentally all the same.

The best managers think of themselves as playing coaches. They should be the first on the field in the morning and the last to leave it at night. They're available to their players seven days a week from 8 a.m. to 11 p.m. In the business context, being there on the scene and available is a simple necessity—an if-not-forget-it. Timing is everything. If the manager isn't there when he's needed—to supply the blessing or the go-ahead or the missing piece of a puzzle—his people will lose satisfaction, then interest and zeal.

A good manager is a blocking back whenever and wherever needed. No job is too menial for him if it helps one of his players advance toward his objective. How many times has a critical project been held up because there was no one around who could get someone out of bed, or type up a fresh draft, or run off some copies on the Xerox. A good manager carries his players' home phone numbers with him and has an understanding with them that, just as he is available to them until eleven o'clock any night, so they are available to him on the same terms.

Like a good coach, he protects his players from unreasonable demands of the owners. In business, he identifies company objectives and gets his players to see them as their objectives. Then he gets "top" management to agree to the objectives. Once this is done, he is able to be hard-nosed with "top" management whenever they try to distract him or his players.

"Top" managements are easily panicked when the organization is having a lean year. If the chief executive doesn't calm them down they can blow hither and yon and hot and cold. Under these conditions they must be constantly and forcefully told off when they suggest something or try something that not only doesn't help the chief and his team, but actually sets them back.

A good * "top" management should read the monthly reports, meet quarterly with the chief executive, and function as his sounding board. For these duties, they should be paid less than, not more than, key division and department heads. The Establishment in any field seldom earns its pay.

---

* I must take it on faith that there are good "top" managements: I've just never seen one.

MANAGEMENT CONSULTANTS

The effective ones are the one-man shows. The institutional ones are disastrous. They waste time, cost money, demoralize and distract your best people, and don't solve problems. They are people who borrow your watch to tell you what time it is and then walk off with it.

Don't use them under any circumstances. Not even to keep your stockholders and directors quiet. It isn't worth it.

Many organizations who've been through it will react promptly, thoroughly, and effectively to the threat: "If you fellows don't get shaped up in thirty days so you're a credit to the rest of the company, I'm going to call in Booz, Allen."

MARKETING

"Marketing" departments—like planning departments, personnel departments, management development departments, advertising departments, and public relations departments—are usually camouflage designed to cover up for lazy or worn-out chief executives.

Marketing, in the fullest sense of the word, is the name of the game. So it had better be handled by the boss and his line, not by staff hecklers. Once or twice a year for three or four days the boss takes ten, twenty, or thirty of his key people, including some from the ad agency and the controller's office, away to some secluded spot. On average they spend twelve hours a day asking unaskable questions, rethinking the business (What are we selling? To whom? At what prices? How do we get to him? In what form?), four hours a day relaxing and exercising, and eight hours a day sleeping. It's hard work. But more good marketing changes will come out of such meetings than out of any year-round staff department of "experts" with "marketing" signs on the door.

MARS, MAN FROM

In solving a complex problem, pretend that you are a
Martian. Assume that you understand everything about
Man and his Society — except what has been done in the
past by other companies in your industry to solve this
particular problem.

For example, when the Massachusetts Turnpike Authority
was about to tear down the Avis headquarters in Boston,
we asked ourselves, "Where would a man from Mars
locate the headquarters of an international company in
the business of renting and leasing vehicles without
drivers?" The main criteria became clear: near active
domestic and international airports, so we could go see
our managers and they could get to us; and in a good
accounting and clerical labor market. So we moved to
Long Island between JFK and LaGuardia, while our
larger competition isolated itself on the tight little island
of Manhattan.

MEETINGS

Generally speaking, the fewer the better. Both as to the number of meetings and the number of participants.

There are several kinds of useful meetings. Here are a couple:

The Weekly Staff Meeting
Purpose: information, not problem-solving.
For: all division and department heads.
Takes place same time same place, like TV news.
Starts *on the dot no matter who's missing*.
Goes around the room: reports on problems, developments
(a crossed wire is handled by Joe saying to Pete: "I'll see
you after the meeting on that"). A number of people
should and will say "Pass."
Ends on the dot (or sooner).
No attendance taken.
No notice of meeting sent in advance.
No stigma for non-attendance.
One-page minutes dictated, typed, *and* circulated the
same day.*

* The chief ought to write this. In the worst companies, the chief's
assistant-to does it, and undoes all the trust created by the meeting.

Every six months have a secret ballot—"Do we *need* a weekly staff meeting?"

The Problem- (or Opportunity-) Focused Meeting

Shouldn't happen more than a few times a year after a company gets going. A good manager with a nose for when an important problem or opportunity is facing his group earns his salt by calling this meeting. In my experience it's really a series of meetings.

After the first session, some are against, some are for, some think it's all a waste of time. I usually try to pick out a well-respected operating man who is reasonably enthusiastic for the idea and pair him with an assistant controller. They are glad to come back in a week to report (orally) to the original group on whether the idea makes sense.

After this second meeting the idea is either pretty obviously major (so you ask for a written detailed battle plan to be submitted by your two-man team at the end of another week) or you apologize to the group for wasting time.

Two Meetings Better Than One

Some people absorb ideas quickly from conversation; others respond better to written material. First reactions are best from some people; the next day they're not so sure. Other people shouldn't be rushed.

Once I had a very able and valuable associate who would get negative and defensive if pressed for a decision in the first meeting on anything. He taught me that if it's worth having one meeting on a matter, it's usually worth having a second meeting first thing the next morning. At the first you pick up the convictions of the quick reactors, and at the second you give equal time to the just-as-valuable convictions of those who should sleep on it.

MEMORANDUM, THE LAST *

Use them for dissemination of noncontroversial information. Write them to yourself to organize your thoughts. But keep in mind that a memo is really a one-way street. There's no way to reply to it in real-time, or to engage it in dialogue. Murder-by-memo is an acceptable crime in large organizations, and a zealous user of the Xerox machine gun can copy down dozens of otherwise productive people. The small company cannot survive such civil war games.

When two of your departments or divisions start arguing by memo and copying you, call them in and make them swear never to write another memo on that subject. Then listen to both sides and if they won't work it out then and there, decide it (*see* Compromise and King Solomon). When the conflict between the State and Defense departments was at its peak, it was rumored that 20 per cent of the employees of each department were there just to throw memo grenades at the other.

Memos and all other documents should always bear dates and initials. One of my colleagues once spent a twelve-hour night working on an undated document which turned out not to be the current draft. Why he was not convicted of mayhem remains a mystery.

* *"The letter killeth, but the spirit giveth life."* —St. Paul.

If I were ever again sentenced to run a bank, I promise you one of my first official acts would be to write a memorandum to everybody, beginning, "This is the last memorandum . . ."

MERGERS, CONGLOBULATIONS, AND JOINT FAILURES

Joint ventures are almost always bad. At worst, both parents neglect the stepchild in favor of their own. At best, one parent does all the work, but has to give up half the rewards and justifiably begins to feel cheated. The worst kind of joint ventures are those with a supplier-customer relationship between the parents and the joint venture. Someone always ends up being screwed. Do it by yourself if it's worthwhile, and don't do it at all if it's not.

Acquisitions and mergers are a necessary evil for some companies. Avoid them like the plague if you can. If you can't, set up a team separate and distinct from the operating management of your company to handle them. An underworked but talented President, Chairman, or Chairman of the Executive Committee plus a talented director from Wall Street make a good combination. Let them work directly with someone assigned by the controller. Make sure that all three understand:

1. *That the business will be run as if no acquisition or merger will ever happen, and*
2. *That no one (including the chief executive officer) will ever be disturbed until the deal is in the eleventh hour, and I mean 11:55.*

At that point, the chief executive, the affected divisions and departments, and the controller's office can drop everything for forty-eight hours and, having heard about the deal for the first time, either buy it or kill it. But they don't spend a minute a year on the myriad deals that fall apart on the way to the closing.*

If you have a good company don't sell out to a conglomerate. I was sold out once but resigned (*see* Disobedience and Its Necessity). Conglomerates will promise anything for your people (if your stock sells for a lower multiple of earnings and has a faster earnings growth rate than theirs), but once in the fold your company goes through the homogenizer along with their other acquisitions of the week, and all the zeal and most of the good people leave.

Two and two may seem to make five when a conglomerate is making its pitch, but from what I've seen they are just playing a numbers game and couldn't care less if they make zombies out of your people.
Don't expect lawyers or investment bankers to be objective about conglomerates. Visions of sugar plums dance through their heads at the mention of Gulf and Western.

* Of course your acquisition team should disclose the existence of this veto power before any negotiations get serious. Then they won't be accused of bad faith if you kill a deal at the last minute.

MESSAGE TO
CHIEF EXECUTIVES

Probably whenever Sitting Bull, Geronimo, and the other chiefs powwowed, the first topic of conversation was the shortage of Indians. Certainly today, no meeting of the high and the mighty is complete until someone polishes the conventional wisdom: "Our big trouble today is getting enough good people."

This is crystal-clear nonsense. Your people aren't lazy and incompetent. They just look that way. They're beaten by all the overlapping and interlocking policies, rules, and systems encrusting your company.

Do you realize that your people can't make long-distance calls without filling out a report? Do you know what they have to go through to hire somebody—or buy something? Stop running down your people. It's *your* fault they're rusty from underwork. Start tearing down the system where it has defeated and imprisoned them. They'll come to life fast enough. Be the Simón Bolívar of your industry. Olé!

MISTAKES

Admit your own mistakes openly, maybe even joyfully.

Encourage your associates to do likewise by commiserating with them. Never castigate. Babies learn to walk by falling down. If you beat a baby every time he falls down, he'll never care much for walking.

My batting average on decisions at Avis was no better than ·333. Two out of every three decisions I made were wrong. But my mistakes were discussed openly and most of them corrected with a little help from my friends.

Beware the boss who walks on water and never makes a mistake. Save yourself a lot of grief and seek employment elsewhere.

MISTRESSES

It's interesting that otherwise competent businessmen, capable of budgeting a complex organization, can't figure out that the cost of maintaining two women is twice the cost of one plus certain fringes. An early symptom of the mistress is a sudden surge of creativity in an executive's expense account. I once had a personnel vice-president who had taken up with one of our executive secretaries. If it had been outside the company I wouldn't have minded unless it interfered with his work. But a personnel man with his arm around an employee is like a treasurer with his hand in the till.

Having nothing but persistent rumors to go on, I was dragging my feet until all of a sudden all the executive secretaries got a raise (Thank heavens, somebody said later, he wasn't sleeping with a key-punch operator). But how do you get proof? I'm against using shamuses. Finally it came to me. Suppose it were me. Suppose my boss called me in and told me I was fired and why. If I were innocent, I'd go off like a roman candle. If I were guilty, I'd sheepishly ask, "Who did you hear that story from?"

That afternoon I called him in and told him. He lowered his eyes and asked, "Who told you that story?" He was a good man. I helped him start again a little way from temptation in another company. When I cut all the executive secretaries back to their previous pay levels, not one raised the voice of righteous indignation.

MOONLIGHTING

Like sleeping around, it scatters energy. It usually means that the salary isn't enough to cover living expenses or the psychic income is below the subsistence line. If there's a lot of it going on, it may be a sign that the system has defeated the people again. If they can't release their spare energies toward your goals, they'll moonlight for somebody who doesn't have job descriptions and policy manuals.

MOVING THE HEAD OFFICE

Put one man in charge of the whole operation (let's say his name is U. Heep), and give him the following frame of reference:

1. *All executive offices (including the chief's) must be the same size (small) and furnished with the same basic furniture.**
2. *Don't consult or listen to anyone inside the company (especially not the chief executive) on matters of taste or preference.*
3. *Hire whatever independent experts you really need. But don't ask for advice unless you intend to use it.*
4. *If the building is ready on time, works reasonably well, and the cries of outraged vanity and offended taste die out within thirty days, it will be named the Heep Building. If not, it will be named the Heep Memorial Building.*

The usual practice is to hire architects and decorators and have them report to a committee of tasteless slobs. After taking twice as long and costing three times as much, this method leaves you with one solid result: all your key people are now completely preoccupied with status symbols and have no time for their work.

* As anyone knows who has ever moved a head office, it can be very expensive. From the standpoint of billing cycles and collection of receivables, two moves equals one fire. My concern with sameness of basic furniture is in deference to the timetable. Six months after the move, when the business is out of shock, give each officer the same budget for refurnishing and redecorating and let him run amok if he wants to. If someone feels that cushions on the floor, psychedelic posters, and black lights will help him get his job done, I'm all for it. For further philosophy on offices, *see* Telephone Operators.

N NEPOTISM, THE SMELL OF

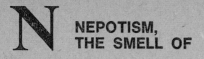

The fatal fact about nepotism is that the really good
people won't go to work for you in the first place or will
quit or quit trying for your job when they spot your
uncle, brother, nephew, wife, mistress, or son on the
payroll. They can't expect a fair shake if you're getting
breakfast news from a special source.

And what nepotists can't seem to understand is that it
doesn't matter whether they're playing family favorites or
not. Or even how good the relative is. If there's even a
bare possibility that you're prejudiced, the smell of it
will scare off or turn off the very people you need most.
The stockholders will never know how many good people
they missed who never applied for the job.

One odd thing about nepotism is that people with strong
Calvinist tendencies are often hardest to persuade. The
molecular biologist working long hours for low pay to
cure cancer has his wife working as a lab technologist.
When questioned, he says, "I'd have to pay twice as much
for someone half as good." He misses the point. If she
ever cuts a corner because she's thinking of the salad

for dinner or the baby's formula, the rest of the lab staff will catch the infection. To them, she's the boss's wife.

"But my brother is the best salesman in the business," says the sales manager. Then let him prove it somewhere else. If he's that good, it's not fair to him to stay under you where he'll never know for sure how good he is.

Nepotism is a way of screwing the non-family share-holders. If all the shareholders are family, then it doesn't matter : they're only screwing each other. But when Ford Motor Company stock was sold to the public, Henry II and his brothers should have gotten out of the management. When they didn't, it seemed inevitable that their first classic misadventure should turn out to be named after a relative.

In the old world, nepotism worked fine for the Rothschilds.

It won't work in the new world for anybody.

If the company's economic and financial position is weak, the results of nepotism can show up fast. Gerry Eskow succeeded his father as president of Yale Express in 1960. Five years later the company went bankrupt.

In rich companies built on an important share of an oligopoly, nepotism will take longer to work its woe.

But two or three more generations of Fords, Sarnoffs, and Watsons in charge may well suffice to kill Ford, RCA, and IBM just as dead as little Yale Express.

NO-NO'S

Reserved parking spaces.   If you're so bloody important, you better be first one in the office. Besides, you'll meet a nice class of people in the employee's parking lot.

Special-quality stationery   for the boss and his elite.

Muzak,   except in the areas where the work is only suitable for mental defectives.

Bells and buzzers   (even telephones can be made to signal with lights).

Company shrinks.   Unless it's really optional, and the shrink reports only to the patient, and suitable precautions have been taken to make sure the personnel department can't tap into the data.

Outside directorships and trusteeships   for the chief executive. Give up all those non-jobs. You can't even run your own company, dummy.

Company plane.   It's just a variation of the company-paid golf club, and the big office with three secretaries. Another line drawn through the company between the Brahmins and the untouchables. And the plane's always in Palm Beach, Augusta, Aspen, or Las Vegas when the business needs it. Best thing about it: if it has only one pilot, someday he'll get ptomaine with a whole load of "top" management aboard ...

Manager's Monthly.   Or any other time-consuming report imposed on the troops by "top" management. It's a joke because it consumes ten pounds of energy to produce each ounce of misunderstanding.

Except in poker, bridge, and similar play-period activities, **don't con anybody.**

Not your wife
Not your children
Not your employees
Not your customers
Not your stockholders
Not your boss
Not your associates
Not your suppliers
Not your regulatory authorities
Not even your competitors

Don't con yourself either.

Social relations within the firm.   Okay with your peers. But not with people who report to you. You'll inevitably see more of the ones you like — and they may not be the best performers. Your own performance depends on your ability to be just. Don't make it any tougher than it is.

Hiring.   To keep an organization young and fit, don't hire anyone until everybody's so overworked they'll be glad to see the newcomer no matter where he sits.

Trade associations — as a chance to fix prices, and allocate customers and markets with your friendly competitors. Antitrust laws are different: you're not innocent until proven guilty. If all your customers are north of Main Street and all your competitor's customers are south of Main Street, you're both guilty by inference. And nobody has to prove the two of you ever communicated in any way. Treble damages. Jail. So watch it, bubele.

Conventions. The public relations dream: much money, time, and energy signifying nothing. The best way is to ignore them. The next best way is to send one line man (rotate the assignment like kitchen police). On his return, ask him to make a thirty-second all-inclusive oral report to the weekly staff meeting covering everything of significance that he heard, saw, and learned. The worst way is to give your P.R. department a blank check and tell them to make a big splash.

House organs. Spend the money making stockholders out of your employees and then sending them (along with the other stockholders) honest reports on how the company's really doing: good and bad. Reading a house organ is like going down in warm maple syrup for the third time.

Greed. To increase our share of the market a few years ago, I was on the verge of approving the start-up of a new subsidiary — which would compete with our bread-and-butter business — at discount prices. To verify my own brilliance I tried the idea out on a tall, rangy regional vice-president named Stepnowski. After hearing the plan described in some detail, he sank the whole project with one sentence: "I don't know what *you* call it, but we Polacks call that 'pissing in the soup'."

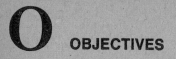

O OBJECTIVES

One of the important functions of a leader is to make the organization concentrate on its objectives. In the case of Avis, it took us six months to define one objective — which turned out to be: "We want to become the fastest-growing company with the highest profit margins in the business of renting and leasing vehicles without drivers."

That objective was simple enough so that we didn't have to write it down. We could put it in every speech and talk about it wherever we went. And it had some social significance, because up to that time Hertz had a crushingly large share of the market and was thinking and acting like General Motors.

It also included a definition of our business: "renting and leasing vehicles without drivers". This let us put the blinders on ourselves and stop considering the acquisition of related businesses like motels, hotels, airlines, and travel agencies. It also showed us that we had to get rid of some limousine and sightseeing companies that we already owned.

Once these objectives are agreed on, the leader must be merciless on himself and on his people. If an idea that pops into his head or out of their mouths is outside the objective of the company, he kills it without trial.

Peter Drucker was never more right than when he wrote: "Concentration is the key to economic results ... no other principle of effectiveness is violated as constantly today as the basic principle of concentration. ... Our motto seems to be: 'Let's do a little bit of everything.' " *

It isn't easy to concentrate. I used to keep a sign opposite my desk where I couldn't miss it if I were on the telephone (about to make an appointment) or in a meeting in my office: "Is what I'm doing or about to do getting us closer to our objective?" That sign saved me from a lot of useless trips, lunch dates, conferences, junkets, and meetings.

Most of all, work on simplifying and distilling your statement of objectives. Cato boiled his down to three words † — and by saying them over and over eventually wiped out the competition.

---

* *Managing for Results*. New York; Harper & Row; 1964.
† Lest we forget, the words were: *Delenda est Carthago.*

OFFICE HOURS

Anyone who makes over $150 a week should be allowed to set his own office hours. Many will conform to the traditional nine to five but it should be *their* choice. A few will set hours that reduce their effectiveness and cost them their jobs. Overall it's worth it.

People have different metabolisms. If you work better from noon to midnight and your job makes those hours appropriate, you should be able to do it. And if you must have a secretary (*see* Secretary, Freedom from a) pick one with the same general metabolism.

OFFICE PARTY, HOW NOT TO DO THE ANNUAL

1. *Start it at 5 p.m. instead of noon, so the company doesn't lose any man-hours.*
2. *Invite spouses so bosses and their secretaries don't enjoy dancing together.*
3. *Make sure the top brass either doesn't show or puts in a token appearance—underscoring the difference between them and the rest of us playful, indolent darkies.*
4. *Invite clients and suppliers to help reinforce their contempt for your company.*
5. *Skimp on the setting. A third-rate roadhouse is always good.*
6. *Cut corners on the food and booze. Two-day-old hors d'oeuvres left over from a wedding, a tray of Manhattans, and a mystery punch ought to do it.*
7. *Save money on the music. Better than a phonograph is a tin-eared accordionist whose idea of a new number is "I Could Have Danced All Night."*
8. *Kill two birds by combining it with the annual quarter-century-club party. Then all your employees can see living examples (you should excuse the expression) of what twenty-five years in your outfit will do to what were once healthy human beings.*

9. *Better yet, turn the whole thing over to the head of the personnel department and tell him to use his best judgment.*

ORGANIZATION CHARTS: RIGOR MORTIS

They have uses: for the annual salary review; for educating investors on how the organization works and who does what.

But draw them in pencil. Never formalize, print, and circulate them. Good organizations are living bodies that grow new muscles to meet challenges. A chart demoralizes people. Nobody thinks of himself as *below* other people. And in a good company he isn't. Yet on paper there it is. If you have to circulate something, use a loose-leaf table of organization (like a magazine masthead) instead of a diagram with the people in little boxes. Use alphabetical order by name and by function wherever possible.

In the best organizations people see themselves working in a circle as if around one table. One of the positions is designated chief executive officer, because somebody has to make all those tactical decisions that enable an organization to keep working. In this circular organization, leadership passes from one to another depending on the particular task being attacked—without any hang-ups.

This is as it should be. In the hierarchical organization, it is difficult to imagine leadership anywhere but at the top of the various pyramids. And it's hard to visualize the leader of a small pyramid becoming temporarily the leader of a group of larger pyramid-leaders which includes the chief executive officer.

The traditional organization chart has one dead give-away. Any dotted line indicates a troublemaker and/or a seriously troubled relationship. It also generally means that an unsatisfactory compromise (*see* Compromise and King Solomon) has been worked out and the direct solution has been avoided.

P PEOPLE

There's nothing fundamentally wrong with our country except that the leaders of all our major organizations are operating on the wrong assumptions.* We're in this mess because for the last two hundred years we've been using the Catholic Church and Caesar's legions as our patterns for creating organizations. And until the last forty or fifty years it made sense. The average churchgoer, soldier, and factory worker was uneducated and dependent on orders from above. And authority carried considerable weight because disobedience brought the death penalty or its equivalent.†

From the behavior of people in these early industrial organizations we arrived at the following assumptions,‡ on which all modern organizations are still operating:

1. *People hate work.*
2. *They have to be driven and threatened with punishment to get them to work toward organizational objectives.*
3. *They like security, aren't ambitious, want to be told what to do, dislike responsibility.*

* By all the evidence, the other industrialized countries are as bad off, but no worse; their major institutions are operated on the same silly assumptions.
† Dismissal and blacklisting brought starvation to an industrial worker; excommunication brought the spiritual equivalent of death to a churchgoer.
‡ Douglas McGregor (*see* Bibliography) called these three assumptions "Theory X." Organizations that run on these premises—the hierarchies—are Theory X outfits.

You don't think we are operating on these assumptions?
Consider:

1. *Office hours nine to five for everybody except the
fattest cats at the top. Just a giant cheap time clock.
(Are we buying brains or hours?)*
2. *Unilateral promotions. For more money and a bigger
title I'm expected to jump at the chance of moving
my family to New York City. I run away from the
friends and a life style in Denver that have made me
and my family happy and effective. (Organization
comes first; individuals must sacrifice themselves to its
demands.)*
3. *Hundreds of millions of dollars are spent annually
"communicating" with employees. The message always
boils down to: "Work hard, obey orders. We'll take
care of you." That message is obsolete by fifty years
and wasn't very promising then.)*

Back off a minute. Let's pretend we know everything
man knows about human nature and its present condition
here, but nothing about man's organizations and the
assumptions on which they're based. These things * we
know about man:

1. *He's a wanting animal.*
2. *His behaviour is determined by unsatisfied needs that
he wants to satisfy.*

* McGregor again.

3. *His needs form a value hierarchy that is internal, not external:*
   (a) *body (I can't breathe.)*
   (b) *safety (How can I protect myself from . . . ?)*
   (c) *social (I want to belong.)*
   (d) *Ego (1. Gee, I'm terrific. 2. Aren't I? Yes.)*
   (e) *Development (Gee, I'm better than I was last year.)*

Man is totally motivated by each level of need in order —until that level is satisfied. If he hasn't slept in three days he's totally motivated by a need for sleep. After he has slept, eaten, drunk, is safe, and has acceptance in a group, he is no longer motivated by those three levels of needs. (McGregor's examples: The only time you think of air is when you are deprived of it; man lives by bread alone when there is no bread.)

We know that these first three need levels are pretty well satisfied* in America's work force today. So we would expect man's organizations to be designed to feed the ego and development needs. But there's the whole problem. The result of our outmoded organizations is that we're still acting as if people were uneducated peasants. Much of the work done today would be more suitable for young children or mental defectives.

And look at the rewards we're offering our people today: higher wages, medical benefits, vacations, pensions, profit sharing, bowling and baseball teams. *Not one can*

---

* This book does not come to grips with the problem of America's 20 million poor: it deals with the 80 million psychiatric cases who do have jobs.

be enjoyed on the job. You've got to leave work, get sick, or retire first. No wonder people aren't having fun on the job.

So what are the valid assumptions for present-day circumstances? McGregor called them "Theory Y":

1. *People* don't *hate work. It's as natural as rest or play.*
2. *They don't* have *to be forced or threatened. If they commit themselves to mutual objectives, they'll drive themselves more effectively than you can drive them.*
3. *But they'll commit themselves only to the extent they can see ways of satisfying their ego and development needs (remember the others are pretty well satisfied and are no longer prime drives).*

All you have to do is look around you to see that modern organizations are only getting people to use about 20 per cent—the lower fifth—of their capacities. And the painful part is that God didn't design the human animal to function at 20 per cent. At that pace it develops enough malfunctions to cause a permanent shortage of psychoanalysts and hospital beds.

Since 1952 I've been stumbling around building and running primitive "Theory Y" departments, divisions, and finally one whole "Theory Y" company: Avis.

In 1962 after thirteen years Avis had never made a

profit.* Three years later the company had grown
internally (not by acquisitions) from $30 million sales to
$75 million sales, and had made successive annual
profits of $1 million, $3 million, and $5 million. If I
had anything to do with this, I ascribe it all to my
application of Theory Y. And a faltering, stumbling,
groping, mistake-ridden application it was.

You want proof? I can't give it to you. But let me tell
you a story. When I became head of Avis I was assured
that no one at headquarters was any good, and that my
first job was to start recruiting a whole new team. Three
years later, Hal Geneen, the President of ITT (which had
just acquired Avis), after meeting everybody and
listening to them in action for a day, said, "I've never
seen such depth of management; why I've already
spotted three chief executive officers!" You guessed it.
Same people. I'd brought in only two new people, a
lawyer and an accountant.

Bill Bernbach used to say about advertising effectiveness:
"Ninety per cent of the battle is what you say and 10
per cent is what medium you say it in." The same thing is
true of people. Why spend all that money and time on
the *selection* of people when the people you've got are
breaking down from under-use.

Get to know your people. What they do well, what they
enjoy doing, what their weaknesses and strengths are,

---

* Except one year when they jiggled their depreciation rates.

and what they want and need to get from their job. And then try to create an organization around your people, not jam your people into those organization-chart rectangles. The only excuse for organization is to maximize the chance that each one, working with others, will get for growth in his job. You can't motivate people. That door is locked from the inside. You *can* create a climate in which most of your people will motivate themselves to help the company to reach its objectives. Like it or not, the only practical act is to adopt Theory Y assumptions and get going.

It isn't easy, but what you're really trying to do is come between a man and his family. You want him to enjoy his work so much he comes in on Saturday instead of playing golf or cutting the grass.

Theory Y is the explanation for Ho Chi Minh's unbelievable twenty-five-year survival against the mighty blasts of Theory X monsters of three nations:

There is nothing to distinguish their generals from their private soldiers except the star they wear on their collars. Their uniform is cut out of the same material, they wear the same boots, their cork helmets are identical and their colonels go on foot like privates. They live on the rice they carry on them, on the tubers they pull out of the forest earth, on the fish they catch and on the water *of the mountain streams. No beautiful secretaries, no pre-packaged rations, no cars or fluttering pennants ... no military bands. But victory, damn it, victory! ***

* Jules Roy: *The Battle of Dienbienphu*, New York: Harper & Row; 1965, p. 304.

PERSONNEL, (PEOPLE VS.)

Fire the whole personnel department.

Unless your company is too large (in which case break
it up into autonomous parts), have a one-girl people
department (not a personnel department). Records can
be kept in the payroll section of the accounting department
and your one-girl people department (she answers
her own phone and does her own typing) acts as
personnel (sorry—people) assistant to anybody who
is recruiting.* She lines up applicants, checks references,
and keeps your pay ranges competitive by checking other
companies.

On the subject of pay ranges, I've long held the conviction
that it's much less expensive to recruit from the top of
the barrel by paying top wages. Yet many big personnel
departments in insurance companies, banks, and the like,
consciously recruit from the lower half of the barrel to
"save money". If they only realized what they were
doing to themselves.

The trouble with personnel experts is that they use
gimmicks borrowed from manufacturing: inventories,
replacement charts, recruiting, selecting, indoctrinating
and training machinery, job rotation, and appraisal
programs. And this manufacturing of men is about as

* The important thing about hiring is the chemistry or the vibrations
between boss and candidate: good, bad, or not there at all.

effective as Dr. Frankenstein was. As McGregor points out, the sounder approach is agricultural. Provide the climate and proper nourishment and let the people grow themselves. They'll amaze you.

PLANNING, LONG-RANGE:
A HAPPENING

Planning is best handled by the boss and his key men
(*see* Marketing, for how).

Once I was asked to head up a new long-range planning
effort. My wife listened to my glowing description of
my new job. Next evening she blew the whole schmeer out
of the water by asking: "What did you plan today,
dear?" Bless her.

POLICY MANUALS

Don't bother. If they're general, they're useless. If
they're specific, they're how-to-manuals—expensive to
prepare and revise.

The only people who read policy manuals are goldbricks
and martinets. The goldbricks memorize them so they
can say: (1) "That's not in this department," or (2) "It's
against company policy." The martinets use policy
manuals to confine, frustrate, punish, and eventually
drive out of the organization every imaginative, creative,
adventuresome woman and man.

**If you *have* to have a policy manual, publish the
Ten Commandments.**

P.R. DEPARTMENT, ABOLITION OF

Yes, fire this whole department, too. If you have an outside P.R. firm, fire them too.

Most businesses have a normal P.R. operation: press releases, clipping services, attempts to get interviewed; all being handled, as usual, by people who are embarrassingly uniformed about the company's plans and objectives.

We made many mistakes at Avis, but we were at least smart enough to realize that the professional P.R. operation was as dead as the button-hook industry. We knew too many editors had trigger mechanisms that acted automatically to wastebasket anything starting off: "For release."

So we eliminated the P.R. staff. And we called in the top ten or so people in the company and the telephone operators and told them they were the P.R. department.

The telephone operators were given the home phone numbers of the ten people and asked to find one of them if any of the working press called with a question.

The ten people were given the following framework within which they could be themselves and talk freely:

*1. Be honest. If you don't know, say so. If you know
    but won't tell, say so.*
2. Pretend your ablest competitor is listening. If he

*already knows your latest marketing plan, you use the
call to announce it; if not shut up. (This mind-set
also prevents knocking the competition, which is always
bad for everybody).*

3. *Don't forecast earnings. If asked why not, tell them we
don't do in public anything we can't do consistently
well (and believe me, nobody can forecast earnings
consistently well).*

This system worked well.* Example. One day Ford
Motor Company announced they were going directly into
the rent a car business through any Ford dealer that
wanted to. The *Wall Street Journal* phoned and was put
through to the general manager of our rent a car division.
Next day the front-page left-hand column was heavily
salted with quotes from their conversation.

Far down the page our competitor's V.P. of Public
Relations had pulled off this coup: "A spokesman for the
Hertz Corporation said they were studying the matter."

Hertz was older and twice our size, but who looked like
the industry leader that morning?

---

* It also worked with security analysts and portfolio managers who
wanted to come see us. When one telephoned for an appointment,
I'd give him the rules: "Our next session [we had about one a month]
is on April 10. It lasts from ten to four. There'll be three or four
other analysts present. We'll give you our board room and you can
call in whoever's around of our top ten people one at a time." Not
one liked the idea at first. But each one admitted later that he'd
learned from the other questions. And each had been impressed by
the openness and competence of our people. Yet the time consumed
by us was less than forty-five minutes per Avis man per month.

PRESIDENT'S SALARY (IS HE REALLY WORTH $250,000?)

Every couple of years at an otherwise routine board meeting, some outside director asks your chief executive to leave the room.* Then he mumbles something about underpaid and proposes a raise to $250,000 a year, which is unanimously approved.†

During the months that follow, the chief proposes raises for his various top officers and when the process is complete, they are all nicely in line with each other and with the average relationship between top officers' salaries of all large, medium, or small corporations as compiled and published by the National Industrial Conference Board.

Over the years a sizable and unjustifiable salary gaposis develops between that privileged group and the people who are doing the real work.

Pick out the workers in your company whose knowledge or experience gets you from January to December. Which people could really hurt by going over to the competition? Your board of directors? Your vice-chairman? Hell, no! If they joined your competitor en masse, you'd be fourteen lengths ahead in a year, considering your lightened load, and your competitor's added burden.

---

* Chances are your chief executive sits on his board and does the same for him.
† This whole procedure defies a sound principle: "Board meetings (or any other silly ritual) should be conducted as if Wilma Soss, the corporate gadfly, were present by invitation."

Your key resource people may be engineers, designers, artists, city managers, accountants, mathematicians, chemists, editors, district sales managers, or some of each. But average them all out and they're making one fifth of what the chief executive gets.

Fair? Not in my book. And it cuts two ways.

The salary gap makes the key people frustrated and restless. And as the chief's salary edges up out of the earth's atmosphere, one of two reactions sets in. Subconsciously or consciously impressed by how much he is paid, he either becomes:

1. *Arrogant (since I'm so good, I'd better see that all important decisions get the laying-on-of-hands in my office before they're made). The company grinds to a halt and the zeal drains out.*

   or

2. *Timid (I'm paid this much to make sure nothing goes wrong: so I'd better have a look at everything before it happens). The company grinds to a halt and the zeal drains out.*

Why does the chief executive permit this gaposis, which is so bad for the company? I guess because he hasn't thought it through. It certainly can't be the money. He doesn't get to keep it. He's just a conduit between his own stockholders and the Internal Revenue Service.

Gaposis can be fought.

When André Meyer hired me to run Avis, the last item he covered was my salary. "You'll be paid $50,000."

"No I won't," said I. "As an about-to-be-substantial stockholder I insist the President be paid $36,000 because that's top salary for a company that has never earned a nickel for its stockholders."

"*D'accord,*" said André who always knows when to give up.

When Avis moved into the black a year later, General Sarnoff, one of our outside directors, asked me to leave the room. "I'd prefer not to," I said.

"Why not?" he asked.

"Because if I do you'll raise my salary. And since I'm now overpaid* in relation to the service agents, rental agents, city managers, and regional vice-presidents who run this company, you'll be defeating my crusade for a just compensation system. And since 15 per cent of the pre-tax profits goes into a profit-sharing fund for the top five hundred people, that raise will come out of their pockets, and if I were them I wouldn't stand for it."

The General never liked to be crossed and I'm not sure he ever forgave me. But he learned so much about the rent a car business on the Avis board that soon after Avis was sold to ITT, he bought Hertz for RCA. Come to think of it, we should have charged him tuition fees.

* I was still making $36,000.

Ideally, a new chief executive should negotiate his own compensation on a once-and-for-all basis before he goes to work. That is, he may get fired at any time, but if things go well, he gets no more goodies except those that flow from the success of the enterprise (stock appreciation, for example). This puts him in the position of dividing the spoils objectively among his teammates. If he is the divider and a recipient, his directors and stockholders will usually prevail on him to allocate himself more than he deserves.

PROMISES

Keep them. If asked when you can deliver something, ask for time to think. Build in a margin of safety. Name a date. Then deliver it earlier than you promised.

The world is divided into two classes of people: the few people who make good on their promises (even if they don't promise as much), and the many who don't. Get in Column A and stay there. You'll be very valuable wherever you are.

You might suppose that the higher you go in the ranks of business executives, the more word-keepers you find. My experience doesn't substantiate this. I've been welshed on by a big bank president, the number two man of a major finance company and various investment banking house partners. I only know four people who I'm sure won't break their word at any price.*

* You remember the old story about the philosopher who asked a beautiful socialite at a cocktail party if she would sleep with him for $5 million. She said she would. He asked, "How about $5?" She was outraged. "What do you think I am—a whore?" "We've already established that," said the philosopher, "now I'm trying to establish your price."

PROMOTION, FROM WITHIN

Most managements complain about the lack of able
people and go outside to fill key positions. Nonsense.
Nobody inside an organization ever looked ready to move
into a bigger job.

I use the rule of 50 per cent. Try to find somebody inside
the company with a record of success (in any area) and
with an appetite for the job. If he looks like 50 per
cent of what you need, give him the job. In six months
he'll have grown the other 50 per cent and everybody will
be satisfied.

How to do it wrong: go outside and get some expensive
guy* who looks like 110 per cent of what you want and a
year later, after having raised salaries all around him,
you'll still be teaching him the business. The people
around him will be frustrated and ineffective.

One of the keys is to pick someone within the company
who has a well-deserved reputation as a winner. Not
someone who looks to you like a *potential* winner but
doesn't happen to be fitting in very well where he is.

The organization will rally around an accepted winner,
even when he's temporarily over his head, because in

* Like Bunky Knudsen or Bo Polk.

their eyes he deserves the chance. The phony who conned you into giving him the job will go down for the third time and pull down everybody else he can reach.

PUBLIC ACCOUNTANTS
AND THE AUDIT COMMITTEE

With the controller's full understanding and agreement,
the first time the chief executive meets with his outside
auditing team (including the partner in charge) he
should say something like this: "We want our accounts
to be honest and to give a fair picture of our performance.
No matter how bad. Here's a letter from me asking you
to report promptly to the audit committee of the board
any attempt on my part or anyone else's to influence you
otherwise." Then he should ask the auditors to be
forthright in their audit report. Too often, problems in
an early stage may be only hinted at.

Public accounting firms are expensive. Partners are
billed around seventy-five dollars an hour, senior
associates around fifty dollars an hour, junior associates
around thirty-five dollars an hour. Your audit bill will
be lower if you encourage the controller to get as much
of the routine work done in house before those big meters
start ticking.

Ad agencies love to spend your money on market
research, and lawyers on legal research. CPA firms all
have systems departments and it doesn't take much to
start them doing systems work. With all three groups it
is well to set up some kind of general alarm that goes off
before you accidentally discover they've spent a lot of
your money doing work you don't want done.

The audit committee should be two or three independent
outside directors. Four is a bull session, one's not

enough. They should meet with the outside auditors after the annual audit report comes out, but at least a week before the board of directors' meeting to which they will report.

They invite members of management (including the chief executive) at their pleasure into and out of the meeting. Alone with the auditors, they can and should ask questions that would be embarrassing at other times during the year: "Has anyone pressed you to do anything you're reluctant to do?" "Is there any subject or incident that for any reason you didn't include or didn't give proper weight to in the audit report that you'd like to discuss orally now?"

When the audit committee is satisfied that all material questions have been asked, and honest answers given (whether favorable or unfavorable), they are ready to report to the board of directors.

PURCHASING DEPARTMENT

Yes, fire the whole purchasing department.

They cost ten dollars in zeal for every dollar they save through purchasing acumen.

And that doesn't count the massive unrecorded disasters they cause. Let's say somebody has persuaded a young Edison or Steinmetz to go to work for General Conglobulation, Inc. By the time he's found out that there's no way to get that $900 desk calculator through the purchasing department he's lost all respect for General Conglobulation ("They'd hire Einstein and then turn down his requisition for a blackboard.").

So let's be sensible. Fire the whole purchasing department. The company will benefit from having each department dealing in the free market outside instead of being victimized by internal socialism.* And don't underestimate the morale value of letting your people "waste" some money. If you must, have a one-man "buying department" (see Personnel [People vs.] for the parallel idea of a one-girl people department) for those who want help in the purchasing area and ask for it.

* I'm told that the federal government, with all their joint-use purchasing economies, really pays 20 per cent more for a pencil than you do at the five-and-ten.

PUTTING ON WEIGHT

A sure sign of frustration is putting on weight. Watch
for it on the people who work for you. Remove the cause
and the weight will come back off.

R RACISM

Let's face it. The vast majority of corporations are still operating with dice loaded against Jews, black people, and women of all races and creeds.

Well, it must be clear by now to everybody in touch with reality that it's time to unload the dice. This has to start with a conviction in the chief executive officer. But if he wants more than a scurry by each division to find a company black,* he better follow up his bulletin as far down the line as he can and for as long as he is chief executive. Stamping out racism will be a process, not an act, and the chief resistance will be in the personnel office. It is results, not explanations, that count, as in other business action, and you can waste a lot of time just talking.

* Things are looking up. You don't hear about the company "Nigger" much any more, and the company "Kike" is now the company Jew. Women are still bottom-of-the-heap: "Don't give her a raise: she's making a lot *for a woman*."

REORGANIZING

Should be undergone about as often as major surgery.
And should be as well planned and as swiftly executed.

*I was to learn later in life that we tend to meet any new
situation by reorganizing; and a wonderful method it can
be for creating the illusion of progress while producing
confusion inefficiency, and demoralization.**

* From Petronius Arbiter (circa A.D. 60).

RETIREMENT, MANDATORY

A sound idea for now. But it can be carried too far. About ten years ago, American Express put through automatic across-the-board retirement at age sixty-five. Their travel competitors threw their caps in the air. Seems that certain tour guides, like '45, '59, and '61 wines from the great vineyards of Bordeaux, get better with age. So I'd exempt specialists who have no other people reporting to them.

Early retirement is also sound, to take care of people who, like '51 and '54 vintages, didn't work out.

More important than either is to retire the chief executive every five or six years (*see* Wearing Out Your Welcome).

S SALARY REVIEW: ANNUAL ENCOUNTER GROUP

Once a year the chief executive officer should review all the salaries of the people reporting to him for relative fairness (not performance). Then he calls in all those people and together they review the salaries of all the people reporting to them in the same light. It's an uncomfortable meeting, but it's only once a year. And by doing it all out in the open you compensate for the fact that some bosses are better salesmen for their people than others.

If this is done right, you can honestly say to people reporting to you who bug you about salary in between annual reviews: "Look, everybody is always either overpaid or underpaid. Let *me* worry about you. If *you* worry about you, you'll be less effective and earn less than you should. Concentrate on your job and look up after every salary review to see if you are being fairly treated."

SALESMEN

1. Twenty per cent of any given group of salesmen will always produce 80 per cent of the sales

2. A good incentive-compensation scale for salesmen slides up: 5 per cent on the first $100,000 sales; $7\frac{1}{2}$ per cent on the second $100,000, and so forth. And don't modify it if some hot salesman brings down the chandeliers and earns a fortune. That's what you wanted, dummy. The word will go through the sales grapevine and the salesmen's wives' grapevine and you won't believe the results.

3. Top salesmen (all salesmen if you can work it) should be given stock options and encouraged to think like owners.

4. A good way to kill a top salesman is to promote him to assistant sales manager.* A manager is one breed, a salesman is another. Most good salesmen thrive in the field, wither at headquarters. "There I was alone," a true salesman once said, "with nothing but my golden voice."

---

* A viable theory is the Peter Principle: "In a hierarchy, every employee tends to rise to his level of incompetence (the cream rises until it sours)." Peter's corollary: "In time every post tends to be occupied by an employee who is incompetent to carry out its duties." From *The Peter Principle* by Peter and Hull. New York: Morrow; 1969.

SECRECY: A CHILD'S GARDEN OF DISEASES

Secrecy is totally bad. It defeats the crusade for justice, which doesn't flourish in the dark.

Did you ever ask yourself why there's a private payroll? Or why all wages and salaries aren't posted on the bulletin board? According to the lore of the free-enterprise system money is really a scoreboard. So why aren't the scores posted?*

Of course the company would have a revulsion (or a revolution) if everybody had to look squarely at a list showing the salaries of the president and his nephew, who are paid four times what they're worth, and the salaries of Izzy, Derek, and Susie, who are making a third of what they're worth.

In the case of most marketing or new product planning, secrecy is sinister. It defeats your loyal opposition and protects you from your best friends when you need them most. Secrecy implies either:

1. What I'm doing is so horrible I don't dare tell you.

   or

2. I don't trust you (any more).

---

* I'm not suggesting that you should post salaries. For one thing, it would over-emphasize the importance of money. But you shouldn't tolerate a situation in which you're *ashamed* to post them. Like you are.

SECRETARY, FREEDOM FROM A

For years I had the standard executive equipment—a secretary. Most of them very good. Then I used the Man from Mars approach. Then I didn't have a secretary. Here's my analysis:

TELEPHONE

Before

Jane took all my calls and made all my calls (it really has to be all one or all the other). Two of the many games we played: "How long shall I let it ring before I decide she's not there?" "Shall I interrupt his meeting with this call?" (How many meetings, finally at the nitty-gritty, are interrupted by your secretary asking if you want to take a call, and you never seem to get back on the track whether

After

The telephone operators took all my calls until eleven in the morning saying, "May I have Mr. Townsend call you back?" Then at eleven, they'd send all the call messages in, start putting incoming calls through, and I would do the dialing myself. Result: Nobody mad. (Note, no offense because when she offers to have me call back, she hasn't asked who you are.) My calls were concentrated in a forty-five-

Before	*After*
you take the call or not?)	minute period. I'm on the phone first (one-up). Same thing from lunch until four o'clock, when the afternoon call messages were sent in, and incoming calls were put through again.

APPOINTMENTS

I'd come back from a one-day trip or even a long lunch to find my calendar cluttered with appointments with my own people.	Since there was no one to make an appointment with, people would stick their heads in. If I wasn't there, they'd come back later, or change their minds. Interruptions? A few. But that's what I'm there for.

MAIL

Jane would read it first. What with interruptions it was generally the next morning before I got the replies back for signature.	Had two sets of note pads. One with just my name. The other, for strangers who wrote to the office, had my name, title, address, phone number. Handwritten replies.

Before

After
Advantages: Impressed
the recipients. No files.
Can be done on trips,
weekends, early morning,
evening. Lots faster. The
infrequent letter that
needed typing was done by
staff services. If I wanted
a Xerox of my note, I'd say
so in a note to staff
services.

FILES

Jane filed copies of everything. Just to be sure.
Spent a lot of time at the
Xerox machine or in
transit. Finally had to have
more space for her third
four-drawer file cabinet.

Emptied all three file
cabinets. What I kept
filled half the file drawer
in my desk. When that
filled up, I'd weed it back
to half. If you ever get a
serious antitrust action,
the thing that will hang
you (even if you're innocent)
will be Jane's files.

TRIPS

One of my close associates
had a great secretary.

When I called in the
telephone operators had

Before

Whenever he called in from out of town to get or leave messages, she was "away from her desk". And when he came back, she would have all the mail and memos and appointments spread out so he couldn't find his desk for two days.

After

my messages. The mail-room also had a rubber stamp: "I'm away. Please handle this in your own style and don't tell me what you did. Thanks. R.C.T." They'd open the mail, stamp it, route it appropriately. When I got back—clean desk.

Morning coffee, in-box, out-box, Xeroxing, and other matters were handled by staff services. An important thing I learned was that my secretary had been acting like an assistant-to. Helping me where I didn't want and couldn't be helped. Playing favorites with my associates. I got much closer to the people who reported to me when I didn't have a buffer state outside my office.

Working without a secretary depends on a good staff-services operation (*see* Staff Services [Steno Pool]). And making friends with the telephone operators, which is a breeze when they find out you're going to can your secretary. Telephone operators and executive secretaries are natural enemies.

Build a good staff-services setup and then try to persuade your executives to give it a good fair try for a month

every time somebody's secretary quits, or for however
long she's sick or having a baby or on vacation. In my
case, unloading a secretary worked out like finding an
extra four hours a day.

SMALL COMPANIES

... trying to make the transition to big publicly owned companies tend to make the same mistake.

They look at General Motors and see finance committees, executive committees, planning departments, advertising departments, marketing departments, purchasing departments, personnel departments, management development departments, and public relations departments, and they say, "Aha, so that's how they do it!" And a year later they're out of business. If Alfred Sloan had started with all that crap there wouldn't be a General Motors to look at.

If you're a small or medium-size business trying to make the grade you're going to have to take on a few of the burdens of the publicly owned companies. But only a few. And for that reason carefully examine every new expense and activity to see whether it's a necessity or an ornament.

If *your* problem, like that of General Motors, is to keep your share of the market below 55 per cent and your operating profit margin below 20 per cent, then go and do likewise. But I'm afraid you'll be like the poor lady who

thought all she had to do become an opera singer was
to drink lots of heavy cream — you'll be confusing fat
with muscle.

STAFF SERVICES
(STENO POOL)*

You can't call it steno pool. It brings to mind the dregs of the office. My steno pool I call staff services. And there must be a better name. It serves the brightest executives, including the chief executive officer, because they don't have secretaries.

The staff-services office is luxuriously furnished and the girls are recruited from the ranks of the best secretaries in the area. And paid top salaries.

One of them brings you your coffee, empties your out-basket, does your Xeroxing, brings your mail, poses as your secretary (to a caller who won't believe you don't have a secretary), takes dictation in your office or from your dictaphone belts.

Since there are, say, ten of them for twenty executives, your secretary is never sick. Since the girls are paid more than the secretaries of executives who insist on owning a girl, and since the day goes faster if you're busy (and what secretary for one man is constantly busy?), their morale is high and the pressure is from girls trying to get *into* the group, not out of it.

Please get it through your head. You're not trying to save

* *See also* Telephone Operators.

money. That was the steno-pool idea. You're trying to improve the secretarial services without spending any more money and without having a lot of half-occupied women wandering around looking for trouble.

STOCKHOLDERS

As is well known, the big corporation's priorities are:

1. *Care and feeding of the chief executive, his entourage, and the board of directors (mostly his friends, put there by him to ensure the tranquillity of his reign).*
2. *Management.*
3. *Employees.*
4. *Customers.*
5. *(Way down the line) Stockholders.*

Only very rarely is the stockholder mentioned in a company. I suggest a different set of priorities:

1. *Stockholders. Turn the management and as many employees as possible into stockholders—and with enough stock so they think of themselves as owners.**
2. *This makes the customer important.*
3. *Management and employees are taken care of by their success as stockholders as well as by a healthier company that can afford to pay top salaries.*
4. *In my Utopian corporation, directors are last priority. They are paid nothing, attend meetings because they are stockholders, get monthly figures, meet quarterly for an all-day report on the state and trend of the business, and are concerned solely with putting out dividends and chief executives.*

---

* Professional managers are cautious because they have to prove they're right; owner-managed companies take more chances and their timing is better because it's their money on the line and they have the right to try something they can't prove.

STOCK OPTIONS
AND DEMOCRACY

The traditional approach is that options are for the top
$\frac{1}{10}$ of 1 per cent—for one out of a thousand workers.

Misguided. More of your people must be owners. Your
lawyers and investment bankers will try to talk you out of
this sensible impulse, but the deeper you can spread
ownership the better.

One of the reasons Sears Roebuck is an exception to the
fat lethargy rule of big, mature, successful companies is
that 200,000, or almost 60 per cent, of their people own
35,000,000 shares, or 22 per cent of the company,
through the "Employees' Profit-Sharing Fund". This
holding is worth more than $2 billion: over $10,000 per
participant.

T TAX ADVICE

You ask your law firm to recommend a tax man from among their partners, and you ask your public accounting firm to do the same. You talk to the two men and try to get them interested in your business. Then, as in the choice of a lawyer, you pick the one who will give you his home phone number and who will listen to your problem, ask questions, and then call you back within twenty-four hours with his opinion.

Big-company tax men are murder. They judge themselves by how many pros and cons they can dream up, and how many alternate methods might be "worth investigating". You need a man who will say, "If I were you and had to make a decision and then get back to minding the store, I'd do this."

TEAMS. TWO-MAN— GOOD AND BAD

I've long held the opinion that a two-man chief executive is the answer. Look at the poor President of the United States, and what he tries to do in a given day or week. No wonder our country has been in a leadership crisis for twenty-five years.

But it isn't easy.

The two men have to complement each other, and above all trust each other implicitly. They both have to have a sense of humor and they have to enjoy working together. Each must respect the other's fundamental instincts, not just in talk but in action. If you're about to do something that your partner might be nervous about, you ask if he has a conviction against it. The do-you-have-a-conviction game is about the only way to keep from driving each other up the wall.

The worst two-man team I ever saw tried to act like the Bobbsey twins even though 3,000 miles normally separated them. They tried to keep each other totally informed at all times *in advance*. I suppose the idea was that then they'd share the responsibility for mistakes. But in addition to being time-consuming, this method *reduces* accountability. "Oh well, Bill knew about it in advance and went along with the idea." Instead of, "Holy mackerel, I'm out here all by myself, I better find a way to make this work, or kill it before it gets out of control."

The best two-man team I ever saw started with the philosophy; Neither of us is very good, but our weaknesses (and strengths) may be compensating. Like yin and yang, man and wife. We expect to make a lot of mistakes, but we hope to have the courage to correct them no matter how silly we look in the process. If we do our best, split up the chores, check in advance on strategic matters, and keep each other informed after the fact on the daily disasters, we'll have fun.

Sample telephone conversations:

1. *"If you don't have a conviction, I'm going to do this about that ..."*
2. *"Unless you object, I'm going to take on this [task, opportunity, problem, obstacle]. I'll let you know how I did."* That means I'll call you in a week or six months or whenever it's over. It doesn't mean I'll keep you posted on each day's triumph or tribulation.
3. *"This needs doing. Will you do it? I'm no good at it."*
4. *"Do you know that ...?" "Yes, I'm going to take care of it when the time is right."* Or, *"Good grief, I forgot all about it. I'll do it right now. Thanks."*
5. *"You remember I told you I'd take care of ... Well, this is what I finally did. This is what I should have done. This is what it cost the company. How's that for wasting money?"*
6. In the matter of strategic (expensive-to-correct) decisions: *"I've thought through the XYZ matter. There are three ways to go: the first looks like this; the second looks like this; and the third looks like this. I've got no real conviction but I'm inclined to [or I feel strongly that we should] go the second route."*

In this instance and at this point it is strongly advisable for the speaker to sit back and listen. Often he'll hear: *"It's a tough choice, do whatever you think is right,"* or, *"Sounds right to me."* Occasionally, a good listener will hear: *"You fathead! What's the matter with fourth way?"* I've saved a lot of money listening for that sound, no matter how I cringed at the time.

I've known three-man chief executive teams that worked where two were in one location and one in another. But not very well and not for long.

TELEPHONE OPERATORS

If I ever design a head office, executives row will look like the cubicles of a Trappist monastery, and the telephone-switchboard area will look like a Turkish harem. Money spent on offices for the management is largely wasted. If they are any good it will be apparent to anyone after a few minutes no matter how plain or fancy their office is.

On the other hand, how would you like to try doing the telephone operator's job for a day? Remember, you're the company's first contact with the outside world—you've got to be alert and bright and helpful and quick. You've got to know where everybody is all the time. I'd spend money to make the switchboard girls comfortable. The best operators in the area would be lined up for the job.

THANKS

A really neglected form of compensation.

TIME:
THREE THOUGHTS ON IT

Small companies should be fun. The key people
frequently work six days and all hours and get very
expert. That's a 20 per cent edge over the nine-to-five
five-days-a-week big-business operation.

New people need time to earn their place on a team. New
systems need time to shake down. Lots of people are
quick with the torpedoes on new people and new systems.
Give them time.

Some meetings should be long and leisurely. Some should
be mercifully brief. A good way to handle the latter is to
hold the meeting with everybody standing up. The
meetees won't believe you at first. Then they get very
uncomfortable and can hardly wait to get the meeting
over with. If you have more than one comfortable chair
for office visitors, move to a smaller office.

TITLES ARE HANDY TOOLS

There is a trade-off here. In one way, titles are a form of psychic compensation, and if too many titles are distributed, the currency is depreciated. But a title is also a tool. If our salesman is a vice-president and yours is a sales rep, and both are in a waiting room, guess who gets in first and gets the most attention.

If you find you can't get applicants for menial jobs, maybe your titles are obsolete. Nobody today can tell his girl he's a clerk or a busboy. One airline improved a bad situation by changing "ramp service clerk" to "ramp service engineer". A restaurant cured a chronic busboy shortage by changing the title to "logistics engineer".

* *See* Chairman of the Executive Committee for further thoughts on titles.

TOO MUCH VS. TOO LITTLE

Too little is almost always better than too much.

Space: Too much brings out the worst in empire builders. They'll fill up the excess so fast you'll wind up with too little again. Too little makes you creative in your use of people. Too much puts the company emphasis on office grandeur, not on service and performance.*

People: One person with only half a job can wander around and do real damage in his or her spare time. The best organizations are sufficiently understaffed so that if somebody does something that overlaps or invades your area of responsibility, your second reaction is: "Great! If you've got time to do that, *you* do it from now on." This feeling comes right after the first flash of territorial hostility. Organizations that have time to get into jurisdictional disputes are almost always overstaffed.

Money: A tight budget brings out the best creative instincts in man. Give him unlimited funds and he won't come up with the best way to a result. Man is a complicating animal. He only simplifies under pressure. Put him under some financial pressure. He'll scream in anguish. Then he'll come up with a plan which, to his own private amazement, is not only less expensive, but also faster and better than his original proposal, which you sent back.

* At Avis I resisted demands for more space at headquarters. While we grew from $30 million to $75 million, we stayed in 30,000 square feet. "Double-decker desks" was a common joke. When the demands became too insistent, I let a couple of units move into neighboring buildings. But only units with a profit center of their own. At least there you have the performance yardstick of profit. But let a service function like accounting move out, and if separation doesn't work, they may take out their frustration in empire building before you realize what's happening.

TRAINING

The only way I know to get somebody trained is on the job.

The first time I learned this was by accident. I'd laboriously recruited an assistant (note: not an assistant-to). By the time I'd offered the job and he'd accepted I was pretty sure I had a good man. But the earliest he could come to work was the day I left for vacation. Turmoil! Should I go? For the wrong reasons I went.

Thrown in the deep end, he learned some plain and fancy swimming while I was away. And he developed some valuable relationships in those three weeks that might never have developed if I'd been there. He got in the habit of growing and has never stopped.

If you have more than one possible successor, *never* anoint a favorite. You'll stop the healthy competition for your job and paint a bull's-eye on your heir's shirt-front. I did it once, and the organization tore him to shreds. Better to keep an open-minded show-me attitude toward all contenders.

Every time I left the office for more than a week, I'd write the following memo:

To: *People who report to me*
Date: *Today*
cc: *Mailroom*
        Owner
        Telephone Operators

I've gone away. Until I get back Henry is chief executive officer. Please don't hold up decisions. Anything you do in my absence will have my complete support when I return. R.C.T.

Two things about this. Rotate the acting successor if you can. Otherwise you've named your heir. And don't say where you've gone or when you'll be back.

Remember, you really want them to make some important decisions and some mistakes (*see* Mistakes). That's how they grow.

U UNDERPAID

Some good people become badly underpaid. If you're in this spot, but like your work, cheer up; all is not lost.

Resign. Go to the personnel department. Fill in the forms. Apply for your old position. Under "salary objective" put down what you should be paid.

If your diagnosis is correct, you'll be far and away the best-qualified applicant for your old job and cheap at the new price. When I bullied a griping friend into doing this, he ended up with a 30 per cent pay raise, in a company that didn't believe in paying people.

If they don't rehire you because of "regulations," it's time you left the company anyway, because they've got the tail on the front of the dog.

V VACATION POLICY: GO WHEN YOU PLEASE

Just like office hours, vacations for people who make more than $150 a week should be left up to each individual. No responsible people will abuse the freedom. Your worst job will be running your best people out of town when they need some play time.

W WASHINGTON, D.C., RELATIONS WITH

Businessmen often underestimate the number of able, conscientious, and zealous people working for government in Washington—and Albany, Springfield, and Sacramento. They're usually overworked and underpaid. And motivated primarily by pride and faith in what they're doing. Try treating them that way.

Don't us a prestigious Washington law firm to represent you in ordinary* government relations. All the ready-made defenses click into place when Clark Clifford's boys call up.

But when your lawyer from Terre Haute telephones, it's an event. It's different. They have no idea who he is, and no way of making sure. He can walk in and say "You're my government . . . help me." And they will. And love him for asking. It's a refreshing change for them from the hot-shot New York and Washington lawyers who have all the answers and are telling . . . not asking.

---

* In a major emergency, however, there is no substitute for Tommy the Cork, Lloyd Cutler, or someone of that ilk.

WEARING OUT
YOUR WELCOME

Nobody should be chief executive officer of anything for
more than five or six years. By then he's stale, bored, and
utterly dependent on his own clichés—though they may
have been revolutionary ideas when he first brought them
to the office.

Also, decisions aren't based on consensus, but on one
man's view of what's best for the organization. And that
means even the best decisions make some people
unhappy. After five or six years a good chief will have
absorbed all the hostility he can take, and his decisions
will be reflecting a desire to avoid pain rather than to do
what's right.

In 1940, when Sewell Avery had completed eight years as
chief executive of Montgomery Ward, that company's
common stock was valued in the stock market at $200
million compared to $500 million for competitor Sears
Roebuck. Avery stayed fourteen more years and a race
became no contest. In mid-1967, before Montgomery
Ward disappeared from the stock market by merger, its
common stock was valued at $400 million—a double in
twenty-seven years. Sears Roebuck in mid-1967 was
worth $9 billion—up 1800 per cent.

Lesson for stockholders and directors: If the chief executive doesn't retire gracefully after five or six years—throw the rascal out.

APPENDIX: RATE YOUR BOSS AS A LEADER

Score each characteristic from 0 to 10

He is

1. . . . *available. If I have a problem I can't solve, he is there. But he is forceful in making me do my level best to bring him solutions, not problems.* _____

2. . . . *inclusive. Quick to let me in on information or people who might be useful to me or stimulating or of long-term professional interest.* _____

3. . . . *humorous. Has a full measure of the Comic Spirit in his make-up. Laughs even harder when the joke's on him.* _____

4. . . . *fair. And concerned about me and how I'm doing. Gives credit where credit is due, but holds me to my promise.* _____

5. . . . *decisive. Determined to get at those little unimportant (how they are decided) decisions which can tie up organizations for days.* _____

6. . . . *humble. Admits his own mistakes openly—learns from them and expects his people to do the same.* _____

7. . . . *objective. Knows the apparently important (like a visiting director) from the truly important (a meeting of his own people) and goes where he is needed.* _____

8. . . . *tough. Won't let top management or important outsiders waste his time or his people's time. Is more jealous of his people's time than he is of his own.* _____

9. . . . *effective. Teaches me to bring him my mistakes with what I've learned (if anything) and done about them (if anything). Teaches me not to interrupt him with possible good news on which no action is needed.* _____

10. . . . *patient. Knows when to bite the bullet until I solve my own problem.* _____

Total* _____

* This is your boss's rating as a leader on a scale of 0 to 100. If it's below 50 look for another job.

FURTHER "UP THE ORGANIZATION"

Encourage treason. Whenever anyone says he's been offered a job by another company, don't get possessive. Encourage him to review seriously what he isn't getting out of his present job (and what he is) and see if he can better himself enough to warrant a change.

If he decides to stay, he'll buckle down and work more effectively than ever. The result is worth the week or so of inattention. And your objectivity and friendliness will help him come to a better decision sooner.

You can wince, but if you're genuinely interested in your people, how can you do anything but rejoice if they get an offer you can't match?

Distrust your instincts. With whom would you *least* like to have a nice long shoptalk?

Right. The fellow who's working on about your level over in that other division; the one who keeps getting in your hair.

So go see him. Right now. It'll be the best thing you do today.

Instincts were designed to help us survive the climb from the primordial slime, not to guide us through the day in a modern bureaucracy.

Ask yourself two questions every morning:

1. Who do I least want to see?
2. What do I least want to do?

Chances are they'll be your top priority for that day.

Rubber chicken. You're sitting in the middle of the Waldorf-Astoria grand ballroom. It's ten p.m. and the Great Man is drawing to a close with an appeal that we all pull-together.

Not bloody likely.

For four and a half hours, you've had more elbows stuck into you than a professional hockey player in a full season. You've been fed two weak drinks, four helpings of inane conversation (two on either side) and a year's supply of carbohydrates (you ate two rolls and the baked Alaska out of desperation). It'll take you an hour to get home. You feel like you're coming down with a cold. And now you're looking around at a room full of idiots like yourself who are looking around, wondering how in hell they got roped into this thing again.

Can we abandon these barbaric bores?

A tempting thought; but, instead, let's make them more enjoyable and productive.

If you were a visitor from another planet, had never been to one of these affairs and were asked to make it reasonably useful, what would you do?

Abolish the dais.

Label prominent people (normally on the dais) with puce (for prominent) tags and place one at each table.

Schedule the speech at seven p.m. sharp, *before dinner*.

At intervals, during dinner introduce puce tags and conduct all the necessary ritual, if any. Mostly, however, there should be a discussion of the speech at each table, hopefully enlivened by the presence of a seminal mind.

After dinner, a five-minute break for the departure of those who know by now that this speaker isn't going to challenge or inform them.

Question-and-answer period. Blunt. Real questions. At some point, the chairman should tell everybody that they can go home unless they want to participate in the further grilling of the speaker until he calls it quits.

The times of the speech and the Q.-and-A. session should be indicated on the invitation—and abided by. Otherwise, a lot of late arrivals will wind up with just ritual and rubber chicken.

The business lunch. People seem to be afraid to meet one another except over a meal. The result is that two busy executives who need to see each other tomorrow can't get together for the next three weeks.

Solution: 1. Don't make lunch dates. 2. When you want to see someone, call and ask if you can go over now or later today or tomorrow morning. Invite people who want to see you to do likewise.

And think of all you can accomplish between twelve and two, while your friends buck traffic and stretch their weight belts.

First prize: Two weeks in Philadelphia. If you become an outstanding performer, your corporate reward may be a ticket to oblivion. Not intentionally. It's just because top managements, in between golf games, outside board meetings and charity drives, spend their time assigning their best people to problems instead of to opportunities. If you do a spectacular job with *Time*, therefore, you may be asked to save *Life*. But before you accept, satisfy yourself that the job you're being offered is (A) doable and (B) worth doing.

Lots of stars have accepted mission-impossibles and wound up whistling, "Who knows where the times goes?" in the company cemetery.

Top managements, be warned: After Hercules cleaned out the stables, he slew Augeas for asking him to do it.

Organization charts and rectangular people. Don't print and circulate organization charts. They mislead you and everybody else into wasting time conning one another. Anyway, you probably spend a major fraction of your time dealing directly with people who aren't really above or below you on the chart. Don't let yourself be conned into thinking you relate only up or down and sideways to peers. If people are off to one side but *below* you on the chart, you may be tempted to ignore them, summon them to your office or at least assume they'll do whatever you want. In your own self-interest, to avoid their attack, or to enlist their required support in advance, you should go to *them* at *their* convenience to explain and persuade.

The head of the mail room or the chief telephone operator may hold your destiny someday. Figure out who's important to your effectiveness and then *treat him (or her) that way.*

It wouldn't hurt to assume, in short, that every man—and woman—is a human being, not a rectangle.

The sure-fire Townsend innovation test. If you come up with a new idea for your department or division, you can get an almost infallible reading on it.

1. If everybody gives it something between active indifference and hot opposition, the idea is valid. Also, the importance of the idea will be directly proportional to the amount of passionate opposition it stirs up.

2. If everybody drops dead from enthusiasm for your idea, it's certainly minor and probably wrong. You may be telling them what they want to hear upstairs. And hot new ideas never come from up there.

Campus Recruiting. Send the people who can't go.

To convert a corporate liability into an asset overnight, fire the recruiters and put together a group of the most active, enthusiastic and successful people at work in your company, at all levels. Make them the campus recruiters. Their job: to be honest, not to sell or persuade.

The young prospects will spot the difference. Your man, who is on top of a job that he believes in, will be worth 40 personnel-department zombies who improvise answers and deal in images.

Your part-time recruiters will plead that they're too busy to take on this chore, but it's worth it to persuade them. They'll come back freshened up by their trip behind the Beard Curtain. Who knows, they may pick up an idea.

When their recruiting starts to pay off, make them into an *ad hoc* committee on how to turn the graduates loose on real jobs—to find out which ones weren't turned into sullen slaves by 20 years of classroom dictatorship.

By the way, fire the training department. These baby sitters in the corporate kindergartens can turn any job into busy seatwork.

Money at the top. The best boss to work for — if you can find him — is one who's made enough keeping money (over $1,000,000 after taxes) by his own efforts so that he can walk out the door if he gets pushed too hard from upstairs in a direction he knows is wrong. He runs his outfit like he owns it.

Too much *inherited* keeping money (over $5,000,000) is a birth defect. It produces high and visible insecurity. When concentrated in outrageous amounts, it tempts Daddy to buy control of U.S. Environment Corporation for Sonny to play with. That's not all bad, because it makes a bleeding genius out of whoever follows Sonny. But, in a way, it's unfair. Edgar Bronfman, for example, may be a great chief executive at Seagrams. Nobody'll ever find out.

A family megafortune guarantees a chief executive two deadly plagues for life:

1. A cloud of charm boys will always distort his view of reality and give him a chronic case of corporate pinkeye.
2. The real and total resentment of the poor slobs doing the work will make them withhold the early warnings he needs to get from the front.

Moral: If your company gets bought for Sonny — hang in there. If Sonny is lucky, he'll be out on his ass and some genius — why not you? — will be sitting in his office in no time at all.

Hot air from cold salesmen. Pity the poor salesman. He's out there with nothing but his talent and your product and he has to come back to write a sales report. If he hasn't made it, he has to say why. That's when the worst salesmen become the best experts on product redesign.

They've got plenty of ideas to draw on. No salesman ever makes the circuit without hearing: "We would buy your product if it were:

(A) built sideways, or

(B) turned over, or

(C) painted blue, or

(D) if it included this one simple added feature." (All this is rarely true but it's easier for a buyer to say than no.)

So when the bullshit salesman makes his no-sales report, he must do one of two things: (A) admit, in effect, that he's lousy, or (B) offer excuses: "The whole trouble is product design. . . ."

As product redesigners, marketing vice-presidents are twice as dangerous as salesmen, which is one reason you shouldn't have any. They talk the marketing language of the Harvard Business School, a peculiar jargon full of practical

sounding "unit margins" and "bottom-line pay-offs." It
makes hot air sound like hard sense. Worse yet, marketeers
love to have lunch with the kind of media supermarketeers
whose by-lines appear over fatuous forecasts in industrial
trade journals and newsletters. Any one of these natural
gassers can fill your marketing v.p. with enough random
farts to blow the whole Common Market apart, let
alone your pitiful little company.

The sabotage of free enterprise. If you're going to
function effectively in our organizational society, it's
important that you have a healthy contempt for our major
institutions, public and private—and especially for their
leaders. These clowns are not entitled to the respect they get
as the vestal virgins of our society.

It's not clear to me exactly when "free enterprise" became
a joke. Was it after the Civil War, when big business, big
government and the Supreme Court formed an unholy
alliance to exploit the American farmer and laborer? Or
was it later, when big labor got a partnership? Or when
big military elbowed up to the trough. Or when big
education cut itself in on the deal?

Whenever it was, the heart of the conspiracy today against
the American consumer is the New York–Washington
axis, and our real adversaries are big lawyers, top
Government officials and high officers of big corporations.

When the American system falls, it won't be Communists
who bring it down. We aren't in any danger of being

destroyed from the outside; we've perfected do-it-yourself methods.

Our blowup will come when the American housewife discovers that Clark Clifford arranged for her to pay half of the punitive-damage fines General Electric got socked with for conspiring to defraud the American housewife. He persuaded the IRS to accept the fines as tax deductions. This is the moral equivalent of letting the meat packers deduct as an ordinary business expense the cost of the ingredient they use to make putrescent meat look healthy, so they can still sell it to you.

It's no wonder you can't get senior partners of major law firms to work weekends. I sympathize with them. If I were doing to America what they're doing to it from ten to six Monday through Friday, I'd have to get stoned on Saturday and Sunday, too.

Protecting the guilty. A typical company agrees to indemnify its officers and directors. That is, if I'm sued and convicted as an officer of a drug company for knowingly letting a harmful drug murder or deform a few thousand people, my company will pay the $2500 fine and my legal expenses and deduct them from income (for tax purposes) as ordinary business expense. (Judging by the Allison case, where a known defective airplane engine caused the death of 38 people, corporate manslaughter costs about $200 a head.)

So the Government subsidizes murder.

All officers and directors should pay their own fines and legal expenses, and the amounts paid should be reported in proxy statements along with salaries (now reported) and expense accounts (not now reported).

You may have noted that this modest proposal does not come to grips with the main problem—the double standard by which the law protects a corporate agent from the responsibilities normally weighed against a private citizen. If I shoot my neighbor, chances are I'll be severely punished for my crime. But if, in my job, I'm convicted of withholding information about a dangerous product that leads to the death of thousands of my neighbors, the most I'll get is a civil suit that amounts to a slap on the wrist.

This is because our brightest lawyers have been working for years to preserve the myth (which their antecedents created) that criminal law doesn't apply to what I do as a *corporate executive*; that's covered by the civil code. (In Britain, corporate signatures end in "Ltd." That means "limited liability." The Latins are more poetic and descriptive: They use "S.A."—*Sociedad Anónima*, or Society of the Nameless. It all adds up to the same thing: When the cops come, there's nobody home.)

This legal anomaly has led to all sorts of aberrant corporate behaviour.

Insurance companies, for example, don't disclose auto-accident statistics by make of vehicle, which would tend to warn their customers against the more dangerous cars and thus reduce bloodshed.

All that's required is one honest insurance-company chief executive:

1. His computer tells him that a particular automobile is involved in an exceptionally large percentage of accidents.

2. He discloses this to a few important customers.

3. He gets sued for giving information to some customers and not to others.

4. He loses the case in such a way that, henceforth, all insurance companies must supply data to the public on exceptionally dangerous vehicles.

This is only one example.

Hey, you out there! Think of the most important area where your industry would be serving the public interest if it had one honest chief-executive officer.

Does it alarm you to know that your industry doesn't have a single honest chief executive?

Me, too.

Cutback. When the squeeze is on, call in all the people who report to you—in one room, if possible, so they'll all get the same message.

Tell them, "Don't answer this now. Come in tomorrow with the answer in pencil on a piece of paper, so the secretaries don't start a panic":

If you had to eliminate some activities under your control (not just cut them back), in which order would you eliminate them?

I want a ten per cent reduction in expenses from everybody. No hanky-panky. Don't eliminate an activity by transferring it to a different department.

This is painful, but it *can* be turned to an advantage. You probably have some vital activities that are understaffed. If you can chop fifteen per cent instead of ten per cent, you can have the extra five per cent to feed your starving tigers.

Use this emergency to pull up *all* your weeds. If it's done now, the organization won't go into shock. Give me a legitimate ten per cent expense reduction and plow the rest back wherever you think it should go, or save it until you *know* where it should go.

I know this sounds like the old Hoosier saw, "When they hand you a lemon—make lemonade," but the capacity of people to find answers, if they know it's worth the trouble, has never been tested to its practical limits.

Before you call your people in, make sure you've got the answer for your own office—and tell them what it is—even if it's just a ten per cent cut in your own salary. You can't expect to be taken seriously if you're sitting there with three secretaries and two assistants playing grab-ass outside your office. Don't pull an L.B.J. at the light switch, either— unless you, too, want to be a joke.

Growth fever. Almost everybody subscribes to the myth that a company has to keep growing. "If you stand still, you die," they say.

I don't know which idiot first carved this imperative on the tablet.

If your company comes to a plateau in earnings, take the time to look around and get your bearings. You may discover a whole new direction.

You don't necessarily have to spend your life trying to extend last year's graphs.

The typical corporate reaction to a leveling off in earnings comes perilously close to the knee jerk that philosopher George Santayana warned about: "Fanaticism consists in redoubling your efforts when you have forgotten your aim."

Acquisitions I: How to pick 'em. The best acquisitions will look overpriced and you'll be tempted to veto them on that score. Don't—not if everything else looks right.

The bag of snakes will come disguised as an ever-loving blue-eyed bargain.

Acquisitions II: Lock up the lawyers. Memorandums
of intent are devilish devices that boost legal fees and cut
the chances of a deal's going through.

When two companies have reached an agreement, the two
principals and their lawyers, accountants and other
necessary associates should meet and start drawing up the
final contract—not a memorandum of intent to agree.

I don't know how much time and effort I wasted before
discovering that deals aren't usually blown by principals;
they're blown by lawyers and accountants trying to prove
how valuable they are.

If nobody gets to go home for dinner or if the possibility
arises of having to cancel that Saturday-morning golf
game, you'll be surprised how quickly problems are solved.

If the two groups split up for the weekend, their lawyers
will have dreamed up enough bright ideas by Monday
morning to take them miles apart—even though the deal
was actually in the bag on Friday night.

If everyone stays in the same room, each smart-ass idea
will be rejected or negotiated while the contract is being
written.

This concept is even more important in the present era of
instant disclosure. When you walk out of a locked-door
closing, you announce that a deal was done. Let your lazy

lawyers talk you into a memorandum of intent and all you announce to the world is that if anybody wants to queer this agreement, he'd better get moving.

Don't forget the corporate seals, round-th-clock typists and a notary public. You can't go home until that document is signed, witnessed and notarized.

Brevity. The usual way to sell an idea to a board of directors is to produce a stack of bulky reports in brown, red, black or gray leatherette binders and hand them out to anyone who might be concerned. Days later, when the subject comes up for discussion, one third of those present won't have read the report, one third will have read enough to induce merciful black-out and the remaining third, those opposed to the project, will have read carefully and assembled enough arguments to kill it outright or delay it indefinitely.

The next time you have to make a pitch in a board room, try without notes, charts, handouts or assistants. Remember:

1. Most people with power would like to use it wisely, if someone believable would tell them how.

2. They know that any proposal having to do with their business can be stated clearly and completely in less than one minute.

Why not help them out? When you know your subject cold and have a conviction, make the pitch orally. Stay under a minute. Avoid all props and end with a request for action.

No-nos; pissing in the soup. • Pension plans for top people. Security is for people who don't have a chance to make it big. Above a certain level (you pick it out), don't have pensions. Encourage your people to build their own security by building the company they own a piece of.

• Taking phone calls in meetings: "Look at me, I'm busy!" If you get a phone call from Nixon, how much more impressive to *not* take it. Besides, your refusal will strike panic into those 19 Medusas on the White House switchboard, who believe they have the divine right to interrupt anybody, anywhere, any time.

• Tax dodges. Encouraging your people—with company cars and company apartments—to take their eyes off profit building and focus on tax-saving schemes instead.

• Synergism, a business fad like hula hoops, holds that two and two makes five. Horseshit. Two and two usually makes three, and you know it. Because divisions forced to deal with one another learn to hate with a passion—and find ways to take it out on one another.

• Consistency is something you have to be inconsistent about. With a nationwide franchise agreement, be consistent; if you permit one variation, the finger is out of the dike. But where the advantages far outweigh the disadvantages—such as letting people set their own office hours and firing those who consistently abuse that freedom—you must be consistently inconsistent.

● Jet set. There may come a time when your corporate fame is such that the beautiful people honor you with offers of their services. Decline.

●Liquor and drugs. Don't try to tell people how to conduct themselves at home. But if someone comes to the office zonked a third time, fire him without bothering to find out what he's using.

Do it now. The telephone is still underused. How many times have you read something and said to yourself: "I need to *talk* to him"? You may never meet him, but chances are you *can* talk to him. Pick up the phone. Now.

You'll discover that, in this respect, the world is divided into self-important asses and authentic humans. You won't be able to get through to the former, and that's a pretty good indication they're not worth talking to. The others will be surprisingly easy to reach—and happy you called. Who isn't pleased to learn that somebody out there cares?

But call him now. While the urge is on you. Otherwise you'll just be adding to that giant trash can of good ideas you once had but never acted on.

Polaroid power. If you're responsible for a group of hamburger stands, service stations, banks, nursing homes or supermarkets, where appearance is critical, take a Polaroid camera along on your trips. If you see an obsolete sign a dirty counter or a slovenly employee, take a picture. Show it to the manager. Tell him it will be prominently featured in your rogues' gallery back home until he sends you a picture of the new look.

Worth a thousand words? More like a million.

Mercy misplaced. The average leader avoids prescribing corporate euthanasia for a limping company operation. Why? Not because he can't read the numbers—he's sharp enough with those. Because he came up through a system that excessively rewards the ability to get along with other people.

Mercy may help him get along for the moment. But misplaced mercy is seldom merciful. As a result of his soft-headed decision, bright, able people get trapped in an obsolete division. They bust their humps fighting to salvage a lost cause.

The standard performance-appraisal sheet offers a constant reminder of how far off the track we are with respect to the qualities we need in our leaders. It emphasizes the self-serving skills of the corporate politicians who can't come up with hard decisions that are *truly* merciful in the long run.

"Flexibility," "Adaptability," "Gets along well with others." I don't believe they're what's needed today if we're going to force our institutions to adapt to *us*—which is our central problem.

The Ottoman Turks for over six centuries produced an unbroken succession of able leaders. Their performance-appraisal sheet would have looked like this:

Adaptability	0
Adventuresomeness	100
Cruelty	100
Energy	100
Flexibility	0
Intelligence	100
Justice	100
Gets along well with others	0

Please note—justice, 100. Without that, they would have been nothing.

May I suggest that if you don't start developing your own Ottoman Turks, pretty soon they'll be coming over the walls?

Swing low, sweet supplicant. 1. John Bigdeal, senior vice-president, when he needs an important approval from a regulatory agency, calls someone at or near the top, takes him to lunch, explains in detail and hands him his written application with a friendly request for expedition. The application goes down to Bill Overworked, dedicated staffer, who is enraged at having something jammed into his part of the pipeline. He takes one of two courses: (A) buries it; or (B) works all night building an airtight case against approval, or at least asking enough tough questions so that when the answers come back, he'll be able to ask twice as many more.

2. Fred Humble, senior vice-president, finds the appropriate *bottom* level in the regulatory-agency staff, takes Bill Overworked to lunch and gives him the application. Since Bill has never met a senior vice-president before, that application tends to get his top priority. Humble can now needle it gracefully up the pipeline by calling Bill Overworked and asking whose desk it's on now and then taking *him* to lunch.

Who do you think gets the approval first?

This applies to working with all bureaucracies, inside and outside your company. I just picked regulatory agencies as an example.

A healthy fear of success. People tend to learn from failure. When success arrives, however, they don't ask why and they don't try to learn from it. They go home and tell their wives how smart they are.

Take an unaccountable, unexplained and excessive run-up in the price of your stock.

For years, you've been wooing security analysts. Then one day, they all discover your stock. In a month, it runs up from 20 to 50 times earnings.

That's success! The ultimate pay-off! Wow!

What you should do, of course, instead of congratulating yourself, is call a press conference and tell the world you think the run-up is silly, that you don't know of anything to justify it and that you personally plan to sell some of your stock, if the price holds.

Instead, however, you'll probably accept the telephone congratulations of your directors, and then, in a panic, you'll look around for something—anything—that might justify the new price of the stock.

That new merger you didn't like now looks good.

That half-baked new product line might be the answer. Maybe that big computerization program will cut costs.

Goodbye baby.

Your successor will pick up the pieces. And all because you didn't have the guts to say you thought your own stock was overpriced.

Corporate image. Among the many serious blows American business has suffered, none was more devastating than that delivered by the public-relations man who first applied the word image to a corporation and its executives. The result has been a massive misapplication of national energy and assets roughly rivaling the cost of a moon shot. Grown men who should be engaged in more serious activities have been spending millions of dollars and whole careers on silly speeches, institutional advertising and annual reports that look like a Sunday supplement.

Repent, for the Day of Judgment is never far away. Whatever appeal may be created by a corporate-image campaign will fade fast and sure. The only image you should care about is the smile on the face of your customer as he enjoys your product or service, or on the face of your stockholder as he scans the company profits.

Vanity, all is vanity: The annual report. Take away the words and numbers required by the SEC, N.Y.S.E. and the C. P. A. firm as the price of their clean certificate. What's left? A picture of chairman J. B. Bloat and president B. Lemuel Phat, faces twisted into unwonted grins, congratulating each other on having gotten away with it for another year.

Next comes a few expensive pictures of "operations" with black employees on the job—both of them hauled out of the basement, dressed up in clean uniforms and placed prominently in the left foreground. The numbers and pictures float around a badly written, one-sided puff piece.

If all the U. S. dollars wasted in the past five years on this corporate flatulence had been devoted to rebuilding the ghettos, white businessmen would be lunching in Harlem and taking the wife and kids to Watts for vacations.

But, as William L. Buckley, Jr., must have said, altruism is not the corporate bag.

So here is a viable alternative: Let corporations give really creative support to the graphic arts. Suppose the Z Corporation, at the beginning of its fiscal year, hired a good struggling writer, a good struggling artist and a good struggling photographer and said to them, "We want a 25,000-word report to the stockholders, employees and customers of our company that will give them the absolute truth about us — the good, bad, sad and funny — and the real heroes and villains of the year just beginning. And if we catch you accepting threats or bribes from anyone, you will be summarily dismissed."

Think of it! The picture in front would show the tired but happy bunch of physicists who unlocked the secret of one-coat, quick-drying lifetime paint. And a little box on the page would note the early retirement of vice-president Harry ("Iron Duke") Kelly, who tried to bury the discovery because it would put the company paint division and all of its competitors out of business in three years.

Anybody got the guts to try it? If so, I urge you to make it
a three-year project, with a different team each year.
And don't choke if you have a bad year. Your annual report
may well be the best thing you produce.

GUERRILLA GUIDE FOR WORKING WOMEN

Any Girl Can Survive in an Office.
Here Is How to Prevail. If you're a working woman today, count yourself lucky. The pendulum is beginning to swing your way, and you'll see the time when women (just because they're women) will be promoted over better-qualified men.

My advice on guerrilla tactics for the Organization Woman?

Be yourself. Don't masculinize your dress or makeup. And don't hit the other extreme. Nobody ever slept her way up a modern organization. Don't look for angles or shortcuts. Just get plenty of rest and train like an athlete.

The matter of dress has two opposing aspects. First, there are the many days when you want to be as unnoticed as possible. I wear a cloth cap in Europe when I'm walking around the city or the country, because it's the mark of the laboring man and makes me invisible; when I want a taxi, I have to take it off. If you have a thirty-minute talk to give, a way-out dress can distract importantly from your message.

But there are other times when you feel that nobody notices you, that your identity is in jeopardy. When that happens, go to work in anything that makes you feel good—from flour sack to micro to evening clothes. You're a whole human being, and sometimes you just plain need attention.

If it's your first job, *don't admit you know shorthand or typing* (although they're good skills to have). You may end up in a dead-end secretarial spot.

Keep your cool as you go up the ladder. In business discussions, speak only when you've got something to say. And whatever you do, don't push to compensate for the fact that you're a woman. Be proud of it. You're more fit for the job than you may think you are, because your competition spends most of its waking hours in sex-fantasy day-dreams. This kind of competition is a real pushover.

The philosophy expressed in *Up the Organization* will work for you. Here is the essence of it:

1. *Make every decision* (from your first job as a receptionist or file clerk on up) *in the light of this question:* "How would I do this job if I owned the company?" And then *do* it that way, to the extent that you can. Most of your competitors will be making decisions based on the question: "What will make me look good to my boss?" or "What does my boss want me to do?" or even "What exactly did he tell me to do?" None of these questions will lead to effective action.

2. *Fight nonsense.* All organizations are at least 50 per cent waste—waste people, waste effort, waste space, and waste time. But keep cool. You can't change it all overnight. When asked, or when you get a chance, strike a blow against nonsense—no matter how entrenched and popular it may be.

---

3. *Fight for justice.* There won't be much of it in your organization. Many of the people will be fantastically overpaid or underpaid for what they contribute. Just make mental notes as you go up the organization. Ask yourself every so often: "Have I sold out my fellow man yet!" (Or woman.) The giant organizations have lots of money and power to corrupt you with, which brings us to the most misunderstood part of it all:

4. *You don't have to abandon or compromise your principles in order to succeed in organizations.* The reason for this is that everybody else is so busy selling out, or has sold out so often, that when *you* come along and *don't* sell out or compromise, you stand out immediately.

5. *Have fun.* Don't underestimate the value of fun in making organizations effective.

NO-NO'S

Women's Lib. There is a series of *real* revolutions under way. But the Women's Liberationists are the female equivalents of bomb-throwing TV-freaks like Abbie Hoffman and Jerry Rubin. They're just the lunatic fringe. And they're contraproductive. The one thing the Establishment is prepared for is violent frontal attack. They may have pure lard inside, but they've got twenty-four inches of armor plate in front. Which is why the real action will be *inside* the institutions for corporate guerrillas like you, and *outside* them for the masters of fact and public-opinion pressure like Ralph Nader.

Office politics. Don't waste the time and energy. If you concentrate quietly on the as-if-you-owned-the-company framework for making decisions, you'll stand out in the crowd. Remember that power-mad corporate politicians usually get their heads removed somewhere along the line.

Nepotism. If the top boy has his son-in-law, his nephew, and his cousin on the payroll, forget it. Nepotism is like cancer, and you want to join a healthy body.

Avoid banks, insurance companies, and other backward industries. These have long been refuges for security-oriented, country-club-joining, martini-drinking time servers.

Machiavellian self-promoting strategies. Every success I've ever had came about because I was trying to help other people. *Up the Organization* was written to help a group of friends who were starting off in business together. Every promotion I got at American Express came about when I was up to my ears helping my associates be as effective as possible while having as much fun as possible. On the other hand, every time I had a really clever idea for making *me* a lot of money or for getting *me* into some interesting job, it turned out to be an utter failure.

Blubbering thanks. Don't be effusive when you thank your boss for a raise or a promotion. Quietly remind him you expect to be considered for every future opening on the basis of your ability and record.

Look up every two years or so to see how you're doing. If you're not moving fast enough, start looking for another job. Or break off with a few discontented colleagues and form your own firm. Mary Wells, one of advertising's most phenomenal successes, moved a couple of times before she started her own firm. But don't quit until you've got that other job. Personnel departments, like banks, deal only with people who don't need them.

When you get farther along, remember Leo Rosten's maxim: "First-rate people hire first-rate people; second-rate people hire third-rate people." Hire the best you can. Whenever I hired anybody, I'd ask myself: "How would I like to work for him—or her—someday?" The nod will go to the one I'd rather work for. This question is a real sleeper. It gets to such issues as: Are you protecting yourself against potential threats, or are you trying to get the best people you can? It also gets to the root of leadership. Once you've hired those assistants, if you're a true leader, you *will* be working for them—to help them become the best they can be.

Finally—and this may be a rough test—when you get your first big job, find the worst apple in your new barrel and fire him (or her). Any time within the first ninety days will be all right. Don't rush, don't push, and don't have an unnecessary bloodbath. But people in organizations have long embraced the myth that women can't bring themselves to do certain dirty jobs that have to be done. And firing people is often important.

Good luck. This is the dawning of the Age of Artemis—Diana, goddess of the hunt. And when it's in full bloom, I hope to God it's characterized by people working together—and having fun doing it—in organizations that are just.

Robert Townsend Answers Questions:
What Do You Do If —

Q — The man in the office next to you, who does
pretty much what you do, is getting 50 per cent more
salary.

You wait until your boss compliments you for some job.
Then quietly make your points: "Thanks, but my paycheck
will reflect whether I'm appreciated or not. I know men
get paid more for doing what I'm doing. My aim is to turn
in a performance that will put me in the top salary
bracket of all people doing my work — male and female.
I'm not going to accept a discount because I'm a woman.
But, as I said — thanks for the compliment."

Q — Your boss (male) is leaving. You're qualified
for the job, but they'll consider only a man.

Tell your boss that you're available and expect to be
considered. If you're passed over because you're a woman,
get a job with another company.

Q — You've arrived as a top executive and you are
the only woman at the board meeting. The chairman
asks you to take notes.

Do it. But no matter how long the meeting, the minutes you
produce should be one page. (I know of one woman who
went this route and almost took over the company.)

Q — Your job has grown to include occasional overnight travel. Your husband and kids feel this cuts into their time.

Your husband is lying about how the kids feel. Ask them. Then ask yourself what makes your heart leap. Then divorce your husband or your job. Take into consideration that good jobs are scarce and men are a dime a dozen.

Q — Your husband calls and tells you to drop everything and meet him for a drink at four. He's just landed a big account, and after all, he earns more money than you — he sees your job as an indulgence.

Don't go. Be nice. Congratulate him. Give him full ego massage that night. But next week, straighten him out about your job.

Q — You're invited to business parties, but aren't asked to bring your husband.

Great! Don't.

Q — The men in the office are beginning to think of you as one of the boys. You like equality, but don't like blue jokes.

If you're surrounded by witless slobs, join another company.

Q—You've been promoted over the head of a man
—or several men—in your office.

Keep cool. Play it straight.

Q—Something goes wrong at home. Your husband
expects you to take the day off to attend to it. His
job is more important.

*If it's a serious emergency, you'll want to stay home, and
you should. If it's just your husband putting you down,
straighten him out.*

Q—The man in power makes a pass.
*Any airline hostess can give you seventeen ways to
say no without making him mad or putting him down.*

Q—You're surrounded by male colleagues—all
suspicious, or terrified, of tears—and you can't
help busting out crying.

*You're entitled to burst into tears once per career. More
than that, and your self-control (an executive quality not
to be dismissed lightly) is in doubt. How about developing
a set of honest exit lines (leaving the room with icy calm):
"Excuse me, please. I'm so mad I'm about to—" (fill in
the blank yourself).*

ACKNOWLEDGMENTS

Having no secretary and an unreadable hand, I was doubly blessed with the unfailing help of Starr Johnson (Moonlight West) and Angie Abbatello (Moonlight East). Thank you.

David Dushkin steered me to Bob Gottlieb and Tony Schulte at Knopf, for which I'm grateful: when you have to deal with a stark raving mad industry like book publishing, it's well to deal directly with the head lunatics. Emmet Hughes and Lew Estrin gave valuable thinking and criticism, for which I thank them.

T. George Harris gave invaluable encouragement and help before and during the writing. It's perfectly safe to say that if he hadn't been around to push, the book wouldn't have been written.

It would be unthinkable not to mention the educational value of my fourteen years at American Express. During those years (1948–62) the company was rich enough to do—and did—almost everything wrong. In that near-perfect learning environment I formed the valuable habit of observing what action was taken, considering the *opposite* course, and then working back, when necessary, to what really made sense.

For the past ten years, Donald Petrie and Jerry Hardy, two voices laughing hysterically in the institutional wilderness, have kept telling me that just because we were alone didn't mean that we were wrong. Without their ideas and reinforcement, I'd have probably given up before the conclusive (to us) opportunity to test this pattern of management came along.

☐ 14812 8   **INVESTMENT**   W. L. B. Fairweather   30p

Gilt-edged; debenture stocks; price-earnings ratio; loan stocks—if you are not fully conversant with the meaning of these and many other phrases and have money-making aspirations, this book has been written for you.

A lucid, easy-to-understand exposition of the financial machinery which runs our free enterprise economy, it will help those who already have capital invested and would like to talk to their broker in his own language, and those who are considering taking the plunge (you may have no money at all to invest but would simply like to read and understand the City Page in your newspaper).

All who read this book will gain a further understanding of how to make the best use of their capital, as well as learning something of the vital role played by the investor in a free community.

☐ 02883 1 **YOUR MONEY** Margot Naylor 25p

What is the best form of investment? Should I invest in shares, in a building society, in a unit trust? What are the alternatives? And how should I set about it? Of what importance is the time factor?

Margot Naylor, formerly Investment Editor of *The Statist* and Financial Editor of *The Observer*, and an acknowledged expert on investment, tells you all you need to know about the subject, whether you are a novice or an expert, a saver or a speculator.

'Shrewd, sensible and wholly practical advice. Very easy to read' *Evening Standard*

'Excellent advice on investment from the best of financial journalists writing for the layman' *Books and Bookmen*

'A clear, sensible guide' *Daily Mail*

'Essential reading' *Financial Times*

All these books are available at your bookshop or newsagent, or can be ordered direct from the publisher. Just tick the titles you want and fill in the form below.

....

HODDER PAPERBACKS, Cash Sales Department, P.O. Box 11, Falmouth, Cornwall.

Please send cheque or postal order, no currency, and allow 4p per book to cover the cost of postage and packing in U.K., 5p per copy overseas.

Name..

Address..

....

☐ 10670 0 **TO ENGLAND WITH LOVE**

David Frost and Antony Jay   25p

In this trenchant look at England, its people and customs, David Frost and Antony Jay hold up their mirror, so that we can all see ourselves—a race apart, at turns grim and gay, enlightened and bigoted, serious and foolish. And the result is spectacular—diverting and entertaining, relevant and positive. And above all, never dull.

'Witty, caustic, and stimulating' *The Evening News*

'Lucidly and clearly written' *The Financial Times*

'A great deal of good sense' *Illustrated London News*

OTHER BESTSELLING TITLES

☐ 15027 0	DAD'S ARMY		by John Burke	25p
☐ 15154 4	THE MUSIC LOVERS			
		by Catherine Drinker Bowen		35p
☐ 01144 0	KATHERINE		by Anya Seton	40p
☐ 02893 9	THE OUTSIDERS		by Robert Carson	40p
☐ 04349 0	THE MANIPULATOR		by Diane Cilento	25p
☐ 10519 4	THE WALLS CAME TUMBLING DOWN			
		by Babs H. Deal		30p
☐ 12610 8	DARK MASTER		by Raymond Giles	25p
☐ 01308 7	MARNIE		by Winston Graham	25p
☐ 12960 3	CASH McCALL		by Cameron Hawley	40p
☐ 10682 4	EAST OF DESOLATION		by Jack Higgins	25p
☐ 12795 3	IN THE HOUR BEFORE MIDNIGHT			
		by Jack Higgins		25p
☐ 02814 9	CAPE FEAR		by John D. MacDonald	17½p
☐ 02679 0	THE GIRL, THE GOLDWATCH			
	AND EVERYTHING		by John D. MacDonald	17½p
☐ 04461 6	THE LAST ONE LEFT			
		by John D. Macdonald		40p
☐ 10526 7	THE PRESIDENT'S PLANE IS MISSING			
		by Robert J. Sterling		30p
☐ 10875 4	THE SPLIT		by Richard Stark	17½p
☐ 12789 9	RITTENHOUSE SQUARE			
		by Arthur Solmssen		30p
☐ 02934 X	THE COLD WAR SWAP		by Ross Thomas	25p
☐ 12945 X	CAST A YELLOW SHADOW			
		by Ross Thomas		25p
☐ 12961 1	THE LAST MAYDAY		by Keith Wheeler	30p

All these books are available at your bookshop or newsagent, or can be ordered direct from the publisher. Just tick the titles you want and fill in the form below.

HODDER PAPERBACKS, Cash Sales Department, P.O. Box 11, Falmouth, Cornwall.

Please send cheque or postal order, no currency, and allow 4p per book to cover the cost of postage and packing in U.K., 5p per copy overseas.

Name...

Address..

....